Night Science for Kids

Exploring the World After Dark

Night Science for Kids

Exploring the World After Dark

Terry Krautwurst

LARK BOOKS

A Division of Sterling Publishing Co., Inc.
New York, NY

Art Director
Stacey Budge

Photographer
John Widman

Cover Designer
Barbara Zaretsky

Illustrators
Olivier Rollin
Bernadette Wolf

Assistant Editors
Cindy Burda
Veronika Alice Gunter
Nathalie Mornu
Rain Newcomb
Heather Smith

Production Assistance
Lorelei Buckley
Avery Johnson
Shannon Yokeley

Editorial Assistance
Delores Gosnell

Cover Photography
David H. Funk (background
and lower right), Steve and
Dave Maslowski (upper
left), John Widman (lower
left and upper right)

This book is dedicated to
Laurel, Jesse, and Josh. The
long hours are all for you.
This book is also dedicated
to my parents, and to parents
everywhere who encourage
their children to explore the
living world freely.

Library of Congress Cataloging-in-Publication Data

Krautwurst, Terry, 1946-
 Night science for kids : exploring the world after dark / by Terry
Krautwurst.— 1st ed.
    p. cm.
Includes index.
Summary: Provides ideas and activities for discovering what changes in
the world after dark, including the arrival of moths and owls, fog, and
the stars.
 ISBN 1-57990-411-4
 1. Science—Miscellanea—Juvenile literature. 2. Night—Juvenile
literature. [1. Science—Miscellanea. 2. Night. 3. Nocturnal animals.]
I. Title.
 Q163.K78 2003
 591.5'18—dc21

                              2003004388

10 9 8 7 6 5 4 3 2 1

First Edition

Published by Lark Books, a division of
Sterling Publishing Co., Inc.
387 Park Avenue South, New York, N.Y. 10016

© 2003, Lark Books

Distributed in Canada by Sterling Publishing,
c/o Canadian Manda Group, One Atlantic Ave., Suite 105
Toronto, Ontario, Canada M6K 3E7

Distributed in the U.K. by Guild of Master Craftsman Publications Ltd., Castle Place, 166 High Street,
Lewes, East Sussex, England
BN7 1XU
Tel: (+ 44) 1273 477374, Fax: (+ 44) 1273 478606, Email: pubs@thegmcgroup.com, Web: www.gmcpubli-
cations.com

Distributed in Australia by Capricorn Link (Australia) Pty Ltd.,
P.O. Box 704, Windsor, NSW 2756 Australia

If you have questions or comments about this book, please contact:
Lark Books
67 Broadway
Asheville, NC 28801
(828) 253-0467
Manufactured in China

ISBN 1-57990-411-4

contents

go where no sleeping human has gone before . . .

exploring the night side of life

Have you ever dreamed of being a brave explorer, traveling to a far-off land, making discoveries in a new and different place? A place with its own kinds of wild animals, its own plants, its own weather, even its own languages? A place most people never see?

Now's your chance—and the good news is, you don't have to travel far. To get to this amazing new world, all you have to do is stay up past your bedtime (with a grownup's okay, of course).

This book is all about exploring the other half of the day, the part most of us miss while we sleep at night.

Every day when the Sun goes down, the world outdoors changes. Some of those changes you've seen a thousand times. Stars appear in the night sky. The Moon shines

bright. Moths flutter about porch lights. Maybe you've even seen an owl at night.

But have you ever seen a goatsucker? Or talked to fireflies? Or found a moth as big as your hand (and as beautiful as any butterfly)? Do you know how to make the moon shrink? Or what makes dew? Or where to look for flying squirrels?

There are dozens and dozens of entirely new discoveries and experiences waiting for you in the world on the night side of life. So come on; let's stop talking about it – and start exploring.

into the night

Off we go into the mysterious, starry night. But whoa—first things first. You wouldn't leave on a trip to a distant land without getting ready, right? You'd want to learn about where you're going and how to get around while you're there. You'd probably want to pack a few things to bring along with you, too. So first, let's learn a little bit more about this place called night, and the best ways to have fun exploring it.

How far does space go?

What are those spots shining in the leaves?

Who's making chirping sounds in the trees?

What's that weird shadow?

Why do moths fly into bright lights?

How do owls see in the dark?

Why is nighttime so spooky to people?

What do opossums eat?

who turned out the lights?

Just what is night, anyway? Here we all are, having a perfectly good day, and then everything goes dark. What's going on?

Nighttime is actually a shadow— a really big one, about half the size of Earth. Have you ever held your hand between a bright light and a wall to make a hand shadow? The shadow happened because you blocked that part of the light from getting to the wall. And if a fly was crawling on that part of the wall— well, you turned its day into night.

The same sort of thing happens as good old Earth rotates completely around on its axis—which, as you know, it does once a day. You can't feel the planet turning in space, but you sure can see it, because, as daytime goes on, your view of the Sun—which is standing still— changes. That's why the Sun seems to be in one side of the sky in the morning, almost overhead at noon, and in the opposite side of the sky in the afternoon. The Sun's not moving; you are. By the end of the day, your

part of the planet is so turned around that the Sun fades from view entirely (we call it sunset). As Earth keeps on turning, the opposite side of the planet becomes the sunny side and blocks the sunlight from your side. So you end up in a big shadow (now you know how that fly felt). Welcome to night.

night side

day side

As Earth rotates, round and round you go, from night to day to night to day to . . .

how long is night?

How much of a 24-hour day is light or dark depends on the season where you live. Because Earth's axis is tilted instead of straight up and down, different parts of the planet receive different amounts of sunlight as Earth takes its once-a-year orbit around the Sun.

Along the equator, days and nights are about the same all year. But north and south of the equator, days and nights vary and seasons change. The farther you get from the equator, the bigger the differences.

In June, when the North Pole is tilted toward the Sun, the Northern Hemisphere receives more direct sunlight. Days in that half of the world are longer and nights are shorter. It's summer. In December, when the North Pole is tilted away from the Sun, it's winter. Days are shorter and nights are longer. (Meanwhile, in the Southern Hemisphere, the opposite happens: it's winter in June and summer in December.)

About 2,500 miles (1,500 km) north of the equator, the longest night (in winter) is about 15 hours and the shortest night (in summer) is about 9 hours. In the far north, the longest day and the longest night are both 24 hours long!

Seasons Change as Earth Travels Around the Sun

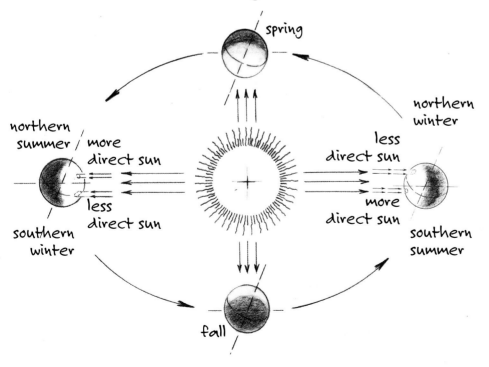

spring

northern winter

less direct sun

more direct sun

southern summer

fall

northern summer / more direct sun

less direct sun

southern winter

Summer, with its long days and short nights, happens when your half of Earth (northern or southern) leans toward the Sun and receives the most direct sunlight. When your half is tilted away from the Sun, the Sun's energy strikes less directly. The rays are spread out and weaker. It's winter, with short days and long nights. Spring and fall are in between, when days and nights are about equal.

Step outdoors on a really dark night and you'll see—well, not much at first. It takes a while for your eyes to adjust. After several minutes you can see better. But you still can't see as much color and detail at night as you can during the day. What's going on? Why does our colorful daytime world suddenly turn shades of gray at night?

WE'RE ONLY HUMAN

Human eyes are built for daylight. Night creatures' eyes are designed differently, for darkness. So while the dark of night is dark to you, it's not so dark to a night animal. A cat, for instance, can see six times better than you at night. What makes night-creature eyes different?

really big eyes

Most night creatures have extra-big eyes compared to the size of their bodies. Their bigger eyes can gather more light. Flying squirrels are much smaller than the tree squirrels you see during the day. But their eyes are at least twice as large. An owl's eyes are so huge they weigh more than its brain.

eyes wide open

Nocturnal creatures have big pupils to go with their big eyes, to let in more light. To protect their eyes during the day and help open their pupils as wide as possible at night, many have a slit pupil, with sides that can quickly open or close, like a sliding door. Most day creatures, including you, have round pupils that gradually open wider in dim light and get smaller in bright light (see the next page).

reflectors

Two eyes glowing in the night—what could it be? Owls, cats, raccoons, and many other night creatures have a reflective layer, called a tapetum, behind the retina in their eyes. The tapetum acts like a mirror to help with night vision. Light coming into the eye strikes the retina, and then instantly strikes it again after reflecting off the tapetum. Images sent from the retina to the brain are brighter because they get a double dose of light.

The better to see you with: This flying squirrel and most other nocturnal creatures have extra-big eyes for super night vision.

The glow you see in a night creature's eyes is the light reflected off the tapetum and is called eye shine. Different animals have different colored tapeta. If you see bright eyes in the night, you might be able to tell what kind of animal they belong to just by the color of the reflected light. The chart on the next page shows you the eye shine colors for some of the animals you might see.

Animal	Eye-Shine Color
Cat	Green
Coyote	Yellow-green
Deer	Yellow
Flying squirrel	Orange-red
Opossum	Orange
Raccoon	Yellow
Skunk	Amber
Fox	White

color vision and night vison

In some ways, day- and night-creature eyes work alike: light passes through the pupil and iris and is focused by the lens onto the retina at the back of the eye, a bit like a movie projector focuses light onto a screen. The retina is the part of the eye that processes light and sends images to the brain. It's lined with special cells called cones and rods.

Cones help see color and details but need medium or bright light. They're great for day animals, including humans. But in most situations after dark, cones don't get enough light to work. That's why, at night, you can't see color or detail very well.

Rods are just the opposite: they don't work in bright light,

and they can't detect color or detail. But in dim light, they gradually absorb a special chemical called rhodopsin. Once they've absorbed enough rhodopsin, they can send signals about motion, basic shapes, and shades of gray to the brain.

Humans and other daytime animals have both rods and cones but rely mostly on bright-light-sensitive cones for seeing. Most nocturnal creatures have few cones or none at all. But their eyes are jam-packed with dim-light-sensitive rods. Their eyes can gather and detect much more light at night, so they can see better.

animal's eye (side view)

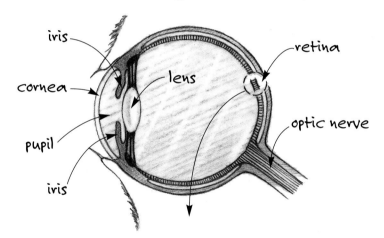

iris, cornea, pupil, iris, lens, retina, optic nerve

night creature

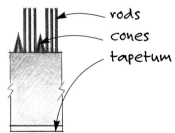

rods, cones, tapetum

- Many rods; few or no cones
- Tapetum (reflector)
- Large for size of head
- Pupil is slit

day creature

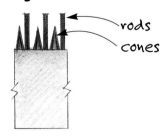

rods, cones

- Rods and many cones
- No tapetum
- Small for size of head
- Pupil is round

pupils as teachers

TRY THIS: Just before you go outdoors at night, study your eyes carefully in a mirror in a well-lit room. Notice the size of your pupils (the dark round part in the middle of each eye). Now go outdoors with a small mirror and a flashlight. Wait in the dark for 15 minutes. Then, without turning on the flashlight, look at your eyes again in the mirror (unless it's very dark you should be able to see them). Your pupils will be much larger. Finally, hold the flashlight under your chin, pointing up, and turn it on while still looking at your eyes in the mirror. Zap! In an instant your pupils contract to a much smaller size.

WHAT'S HAPPENING: Your pupils expand and contract as needed to let more or less light in. It takes about 15 minutes for them to open completely in the dark to help you see. Many nocturnal creatures have extra-large, slit pupils that quickly open or close, like a sliding door.

what color is that?

Human eyes have a hard time seeing color in the dark, because our color-sensing cones need light in order to work properly. Here's a game you can play to experiment with night-time color vision.

what you need

A partner
Index cards
Lots of colored markers
2 paper bags
A dark night

what to do

1 Give yourself and your partner a bunch of index cards and markers. Each of you should put your markers in a paper bag. Don't look at what colors they are!

2 Start the game after being in the dark for at least 30 minutes. Sit 8 to 10 feet (2.4 to 3 m) apart, facing each other, in a dark place so you have to use only your night vision.

3 Pull a marker out of the bag and write the name of the color you think the marker is on one side of your index card. On the other side of the card, draw a big circle and fill it in completely with the marker. Hold the card with the circle side facing your partner and ask what color the circle is. Write down your partner's answer on the circle side.

4 Take turns doing this several times with several markers. Then go inside to see how you did.

5 Surprise! Not only did your partner sometimes guess the wrong colors of the circles you drew, but you probably also messed up guessing which color markers you were using. How many times were you both wrong? Cones really *don't* work in the dark!

something else to try:

Play the game the same way, but instead of always drawing a circle, draw different shapes—a circle, triangle, square, whatever—and ask your partner not only what color it is, but also what shape. Do you think your partner will have better luck guessing the shapes? Why?

make an eye-shine mask

Cats, raccoons, owls, and other nocturnal animals have a mirrorlike eye membrane called a tapetum that reflects light for better vision in the darkness. Humans aren't so gifted, but with this mask you can pretend to be another set of shining eyes in the night.

what you need

Pencil
8 x 10-inch (20.3 x 25.4 cm) piece
  of thin cardboard
Scissors
Craft glue
Newspapers
Acrylic paint in black, silver,
  and copper
Paintbrush
Shiny "mirror" paper
Egg carton
Black feathers, fake fur, yarn, leaves,
  and any other decorating materials

what to do

1 Use the pencil to draw a face shape a little larger than your own on the cardboard. Choose any animal-like shape you want.

2 Cut the face shape from the cardboard. Then cut a 2 x 3-inch (5 x 17 cm) strip from one of the scraps of cardboard to use as a nose. Bend the strip downward in the center so that it curves like a nose. Then fold up the last ¼ inch (6 mm) of each end so that the ends rest flat on the mask. Spread glue under each folded end and glue the nose in place on the mask.

3 Lay newspaper under your mask, then paint the mask black and let the paint dry.

4 Hold the mask to your face and move your fingers on each side of the mask until they are on top of your eyes. Mark the place for each eye on the mask with a pencil. Draw a 1½-inch (3.8 cm) diameter circle around the mark for each eye. Cut the circles from the mask.

5 Cut a strip of shiny "mirror" paper large enough to cover both eye holes in the mask. Glue the strip to the back of the mask over the eye holes.

6 Squeeze some of the silver and copper paints into holders in the egg carton. With the paintbrush, dab a little of each color onto the mask's black face to make stripes, spots, and other animal markings. Let the paint dry completely.

7 Glue feathers or fake fur around the edges of the mask. Place extra pieces near the top of the mask to make ears. Cover other parts of the mask with decorations to create your night animal.

8 Use a sharp pencil to carefully poke a hole in the center of each metallic eye so you'll be able to see through the mask when you're wearing it. Then use scissors to cut the holes large enough for you to see through them easily.

9 Punch a hole in the center of each side of the mask and tie the end of a length of yarn to the hole. Then tie another length of yarn to the other hole. Hold the mask up to your face and tie the two yarn pieces together at the back of your head to keep the mask in place.

10 Look in a mirror in a dimly lit room. Hey, you've got eye shine!

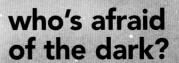

who's afraid of the dark?

ANSWER: Almost everybody is a little bit uncomfortable in the dark. It's only natural. Humans find nighttime sort of spooky because we're not used to the dark. We're daytime creatures.

In fact, it's only fairly recently that we've spent much time at all outside after sunset. Before the invention of the lightbulb, people seldom went out at night.

The dark world outside was a mysterious place. That's why there are so many old, silly superstitions about bats and moths and other things in the night.

By practicing the skills and other tips in this book, you'll learn how to explore the night comfortably and safely. And you'll discover the truth about our world after dark: just like the daytime world, it's a great place to be, full of interesting (not scary!) things to learn about.

becoming a night explorer

You're really good at exploring the daytime world. But exploring the night is different. How can you see better in the dark? What should you bring with you? What's the best way to listen for night sounds? How can you move around silently, so wildlife won't hear you, and safely, so you won't—ouch!—bump into things?

To become a good night explorer, you have to think ahead and practice new skills. Your goal: to be a night creature yourself—quiet, alert, aware of everything around you, and ready for anything.

gearing up

Before you venture into the night, make sure you have the right equipment and tools (and don't forget the snacks!). Here's some essential gear for exploring after dark.

flashlight

Don't forget this one—and make sure the batteries are fresh, too. To customize your flashlight for night exploring, put red plastic wrap or cellophane around the lens and secure it with a rubber band. The soft red light will help you find your way but won't keep your eyes from adjusting to the dark like bright "white" light will. And it won't scare away night creatures, because most nocturnal animals can't see red light.

Remember, though: it's the *dark* you're out to discover. Use your flashlight only when you have to. Keep it off as much as possible.

binoculars

You see *something* across your yard in the bushes. What is it? It's time to grab your binoculars. Binoculars aren't much help when it's totally dark outside. But at dusk and in moonlight they gather light and can help you see barely visible wildlife. Use them to check out the stars and moon, too, and to get a closer look at not only night animals but also night insects. Try zooming in on moths flopping around a porch light (wow, that moth is *big*).

day pack

For stashing all your stuff, of course. (Hmmm . . . if you carry a day pack at night, isn't it a night pack?)

plastic garbage bag

Keep a plastic garbage bag folded in your pack and spread it on the ground when you need a warm, dry place to sit. Cold, moist ground can give you chills fast. The plastic bag makes a good temporary rain jacket, too, if a sudden shower surprises you. Just poke holes for your head and arms. The bag will keep you dry long enough to get home.

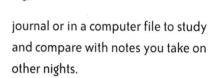

pencil and notebook

You'll want to write down your observations. When you saw that raccoon, what was it doing? Where was it? What was the time? Was it big or small? Did you see its tail? What color was the fur? Did it make sounds? You won't be able to see your writing very well in the dark, so use big letters and don't worry too much about neatness. When you get home you can rewrite your notes in a journal or in a computer file to study and compare with notes you take on other nights.

insect repellent

So bugs won't bug you. Ask a grownup to help you put on the repellent before you leave.

warm clothes

It's … brrr … hard to stay still … brrr … and quiet … brrr … when you're shivering! Even in summer, bring along an extra shirt or sweater. Night air is cool and moist. Wear long sleeves and long pants, too, to help keep bugs away. In winter, of course, it's especially important to bundle up. Don't forget the hat and gloves.

watch

For writing down the time when you're taking notes, and for helping you to remember when it's time to go home. (Always tell a grownup where you'll be going and when you'll be back; see Be Smart, Be Safe on page 21).

snacks and drink

Hey, keep the noise down—no crunching allowed! Choose quiet snacks, such as raisins or a sandwich, that don't crunch too much when you munch them and that don't come in noisy, rustling packages that'll scare wildlife. Fruit juice or hot chocolate makes a great nighttime drink.

camera

A small 35 mm camera with a flash is all you'll need. Film that says "ASA 400" on it needs less light and is best for most night snapshots. If you're really lucky a night animal will come close and you'll be able to take its picture. Remember, though, that your flash will be very bright and will startle all the night creatures around you. Your eyes will have to adjust to darkness all over again, too. So use your camera only when you have a really special chance to get a great photo.

tape recorder

You can take notes to record what you see, but to capture what you hear you'll need a portable tape recorder. When you turn it on to record an interesting sound, whisper the time and place into the microphone so when you listen later you'll know when and where the sound happened.

To identify the sounds, compare your tapes to recordings of night birds, frogs, toads, and insects from your library.

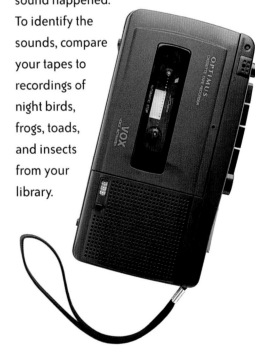

be smart, be safe

Always remember these simple rules for exploring after dark.

- Bring a friend. It's never a good idea to go out at night all by yourself. Unless you'll be exploring in your own backyard, bring a friend along.

- Tell a grownup what you want to do and where you want to go. Chances are the grownup will want to come along, too. That's okay—in fact, for safety it's a really good idea. Just make sure the grownup understands it's important to be quiet and not talk too much.

- Check for rules. In some communities kids aren't supposed to be outside after a certain time of night. In some parks, hiking at night is against the rules. There are always good reasons for rules, so be sure to obey them.

- Don't surprise anybody. Be sure to get permission (in daytime) before you enter or cross someone else's property. Even if you'll only be exploring your own backyard at night, it's a good idea to tell neighbors about your plans so they won't be worried if they see your flashlights or hear your voices in the dark.

- Do some daytime scouting. During the day, check out the place you'll be exploring at night. How long does it take you to get there? Where will you sit to watch for birds or animals? Are there thorny bushes, or rocks or sticks you might trip over, or other places you'll want to avoid?

- Come equipped. Gather together the tools and equipment you just read about on pages 18 through 20. At the very least, be sure to have a flashlight with fresh batteries, a long-sleeved warm shirt or jacket, and a wristwatch.

- Don't forget to use insect repellent. Mosquitoes and other biting bugs are hungriest at sunset and in the early evening, the same times you'll probably be doing most of your night exploring. Ask a grownup to help you choose the right kind (some repellents are just for adults) and show you how to use it.

- Walk slowly and carefully. What goes bump in the night? Maybe *you*—if you forget that you can't see as far ahead of you as usual (even with a flashlight). Watch where you put your feet, and be ready to stop fast. Remember, you're a daytime creature in a nighttime world.

- Stay away from streets, roads, and traffic as much as possible. It's hard for drivers to see at night, too. If you must walk near a street, turn on your flashlight so drivers will be able to see you.

make a night observation blind

Now that you're geared up for watching nightlife, you're ready to build a place to watch from. This easy-to-make blind is camouflaged, so you can see wildlife before wildlife sees you.

what you need

Large piece of burlap cloth or old white sheet
Scissors
Green and brown paint
Paintbrush
Paint roller (optional)
Rope

what to do

1 Make holes in the four corners of the cloth with the scissors.

2 Camouflage the blind by painting it in a haphazard way with streaks and patches of green and brown paint. (If you're using a white sheet, paint the whole thing with light brown paint using a paint roller, then use green and dark brown for the camouflage.)

3 Cut four pieces of rope about 3 feet (91.4 cm) long each. Thread each piece through one of the four corner holes and tie one end to the cloth.

4 Cut three or four crisscrossed slits in the cloth for peepholes. Don't make the holes too big, but make sure there's enough room for binoculars to fit through.

5 During the day, find a good hiding spot where you can put your blind. Try the edge of a field, forest, pond, or yard, in a place behind shrubs, trees, or tall grass. Tie the blind to tree trunks, shrub branches, or to wooden stakes in the ground. Make sure the blind is tied tightly so it won't flap in the breeze.

how does camouflage work?

Many night and day creatures use camouflage—colors and patterns that help hide them—to avoid danger or to make sneaking up on a meal easier. A raccoon's stripes, a baby deer's spots, and an owl's tree-bark-colored feathers are all examples of camouflage. Streaks and spots and blotches of color "break up" a creature's actual shape and help it blend into the hodgepodge of grass, trees, and bushes around it. Other animals see the patterns as separate parts instead of a whole creature. Scientists call this disruptive coloration. But you can just call it a neat trick!

Painting your blind with patches of brown and green is one way you can use disruptive coloration. Another way is to wear camouflage clothes. You can make your own by painting grasslike green and brown streaks on an old brown shirt and pair of pants (be sure to get a grownup's okay first).

Camouflage helps hide even large night creatures, such as this fierce-looking great horned owl, during the day.

6 If there aren't many trees and bushes around to help hide your blind, pile sticks, fallen branches, and other natural debris around the outside to camouflage it more.

7 Just before sunset, take a friend and your night explorer gear to the blind. Bring a blanket or a small stool to sit on, too. Shhh . . . now's the time to be still and quiet. While you're waiting for wildlife, take a look at the night surrounding you. Listen to the sounds. Don't forget to look up, too. Maybe you'll see a bat or even an owl.

sharpening your night senses

Most night creatures have at least one extra-strong sense that helps them get around and survive in the dark. Flying squirrels have great night vision. Bats use a kind of "radar" to see. Owls have powerful hearing. Deer and rabbits have super-sensitive noses. But humans . . . well, we're only human. We're daytime creatures, with daytime senses. To become a really good night explorer, you have to learn how to wake up your night senses.

TIPS FOR BETTER NIGHT EYES

Because human eyes are built differently than a nocturnal creature's, you'll never have the super night vision of, say, an owl or a cat. But you *can* boost your human night eyes to see their best.

night vision tip #1:
Give your eyes time to adjust to the darkness.

If you haven't already, try Pupils as Teachers on page 13. See? You have to be in the dark for about 15 minutes for your pupils to open completely so they'll let in as much light as possible.

Plus, it takes at least 45 minutes of darkness for your eyes' rods, the receptor cells that work in dim light, to completely absorb rhodopsin, the special chemical that allows you to see movement and basic shapes in the dark.

In other words, your eyes need at least 45 minutes of darkness to become "night eyes." That's when you can see best in the dark.

That's also why you should be careful not to look at lights or shine a flashlight near your eyes while you're exploring. If you do, your eyes will instantly lose their night vision and your rods will (oh, no!) have to start adjusting all over again.

night vision tip #2:
When you look at something in the dark, look slightly to the side instead of directly at it.

Why in the world would looking sideways give you better night vision? Try the activity here, Disappearing Heads, to find out.

24

disappearing heads

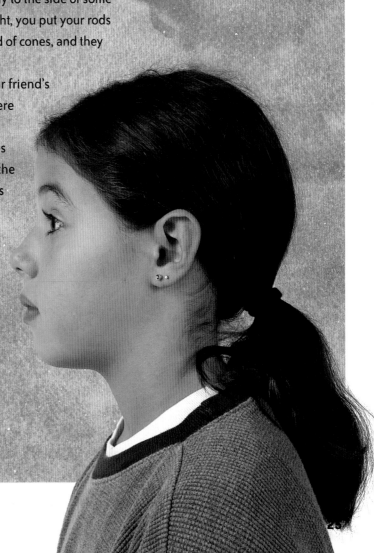

what you need
A partner

what to do

1 After you and your friend have been outside long enough for your eyes to adjust to the darkness, stand about 10 feet (3 m) apart.

2 Stare hard directly at each other's chin and count to 10. Don't move your eyes from the focus point, and don't blink. Nine, ten . . . hey! Your friend's head disappeared (so did yours, by the way)!

what happened?
When you look directly at an object, you're mostly using your eyes' cone cells, which are concentrated near the center of your retina. Cones help you see color but need bright light. They don't work well in the dark—so presto change-o, your friend's head disappeared. Rods, which help you see in dim light, are found mostly around the outer edge of your retina. When you look slightly to the side of something in dim light, you put your rods to work instead of cones, and they help you see.

To put your friend's head back where it belongs, just move your eyes to one side or the other. Ah, that's better.

WHAT BIG EARS YOU HAVE!

Sometimes it's easier to discover nightlife by listening than by looking. The darkness is full of sounds that tell you you're not alone, that there are all sorts of creatures out there sharing the night with you. Every sound you hear is a clue, so learn to listen closely.

To exercise your night ears, find a comfortable spot outdoors and sit down. Now for the hard part: stay still and quiet (if you have trouble with this, try the tips on page 34). Soon you'll start noticing sounds. Some, such as wind moving through the trees or a car driving by, will be familiar. But others . . . what's that squeaking noise? Is something moving in the bushes? Is that an owl hooting? Try to guess what's making the sound. If something seems close to you, use your flashlight to check it out.

You can also boost your listening power by giving yourself bigger ears. You'll be amazed at how much more you can hear. Just cup your hands behind your ears and push them forward slightly with your thumbs and index fingers. Go ahead and try it now (or better yet, go outdoors and try it). Wow, is that a giant cricket chirping?

too *much* sound?

If you live in a town or city where there's lots of traffic and other noise, you won't have much luck listening for nature. But you can still use your ears to help you enjoy the after-dark world more: Push your fingers over your ears so you can't hear that distracting racket. Ah, that's better. Now that it's quiet, you can use your other senses to pay more attention to the natural night, the birds and bats and other creatures in it, and the starry sky above.

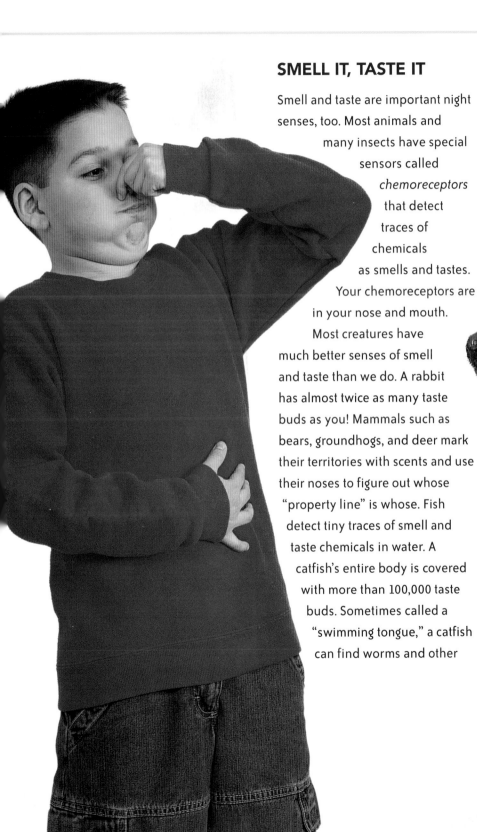

SMELL IT, TASTE IT

Smell and taste are important night senses, too. Most animals and many insects have special sensors called *chemoreceptors* that detect traces of chemicals as smells and tastes. Your chemoreceptors are in your nose and mouth. Most creatures have much better senses of smell and taste than we do. A rabbit has almost twice as many taste buds as you! Mammals such as bears, groundhogs, and deer mark their territories with scents and use their noses to figure out whose "property line" is whose. Fish detect tiny traces of smell and taste chemicals in water. A catfish's entire body is covered with more than 100,000 taste buds. Sometimes called a "swimming tongue," a catfish can find worms and other

food in total darkness at the bottom of a pond or river.

Even though human senses of smell and taste aren't quite as powerful, they're still useful for exploring the night. For example, your sense of smell may give you your only warning of . . . sniff, sniff . . . *skunk ahead!*

27

FEELING IS BELIEVING

We humans use sight and sound so much for getting around that we forget how important feeling, or touch, is. Birds and animals use touch all the time. Have you ever blown gently on a dog's or cat's fur? It instantly turned in that direction to see what caused the sensation (and it probably gave you a what's-that-weird-human-doing-now look). Every hair of an animal's fur, and every feather on a bird, is connected to nerves that send signals to its brain—just like the nerves beneath your skin tell you when and where something is touching you.

Night creatures use touch to help them find their way in the dark. Some navigate by noticing from what direction the wind is blowing against their fur, skin, or feathers. Plus, many mammals (cats, for instance) have whiskers, or *vibrissae*, that are sensitive to breezes, nearby objects, and even the movements of other animals. Earthworms have tiny hairs called *setae* that feel the vibrations caused by moles digging for a wormy meal.

As a night explorer, your sense of touch is important for helping you be more aware of your surroundings. To discover how useful touch can be, try "That's My Tree!" on the next page.

that's my tree!

what you need

A partner

A rolled-up bandana
(for a blindfold)

A place in a park or yard with
several trees of similar size
and shape

what to do

1 Choose which one of you
wants to be blindfolded first
(let's say it's you).

2 Have your partner blindfold
you, making sure there's
no way to peek under or over
the cloth.

3 Now your friend should lead
you—carefully, so you don't
trip or run into anything—to any
one of the trees.

4 Your job is to get to know the
tree by feeling it all over very
carefully. Is the bark rough or
smooth? Does it have bumps going
up and down or across? Is the
trunk straight at the bottom, or is
there a bunch of knobby roots? Do
you feel any branches sticking out?
How big are they? Is the ground
around the tree flat? Notice the
sun's warmth on your skin and any

breezes that may be blowing. What
direction are they coming from?

5 Use your other senses, too.
What does the tree smell like?
Can you hear one of its branches
creaking, or leaves rustling in a
special way in the wind?

6 Now ask your partner to lead
you back to the starting point
and take off the blindfold. All you
have to do now is . . . find "your"
tree. Which one is it? Your sense of
touch is your most important tool.

7 Did you find it? Awesome! Now
it's your friend's turn to try.

practice makes perfect

You can't go night exploring *every* night. If you did, you'd never get any sleep. On the other hand, you can't become a better night explorer if you almost never get a chance to sharpen your skills. What to do? Use the sunny side of day for practice, too.

Here in this section are ways to practice your night skills anytime, so you'll always be ready for another journey into the world after dark.

blindfolded "night" hike

Walking around at night in the dark when you can't see takes getting used to. By going on this "virtual" night hike, you safely learn how to use your other senses to help you navigate.

what you need

One or more partners
A bandana blindfold for every "night" hiker
A yard or a short trail in a park or forest

what to do

1 Decide where you want to go on your pretend night hike and walk that route with your friends. Make it fairly short. A walk that takes only about 10 minutes from start to return is about right.

2 You'll be taking this walk again blindfolded, so look now for things that will become even more important then, such as turns, sloping ground, and bumpy or rocky spots.

3 When you get back, choose a leader. Everyone else gets a blindfold. No fair peeking under or over the bandana! (If there are lots of kids, separate into groups of no more than four, a leader and three hikers in each).

4 With the leader in front, each night hiker puts one or both hands on the shoulders of the person ahead, so you're all linked together. Ready?

5 Slowly walk the same route you did before. It's the leader's job to walk slowly and to be careful to steer the hikers around branches and other objects they might bump into. If a hiker loses his or her grip on the person ahead, the leader should stop until everyone is linked up again.

6 As you walk blindfolded, think about how different this hike is when you can't see. Notice how you're more aware of sounds and of the feeling of the ground beneath your feet. Try to guess when the next turn will happen.

7 When you're hiking and can see, you use visual landmarks to help guide you. For example, maybe there's a stream that you know should always be on your right as you follow the path. As you walk blindfolded, try to use nonvisual landmarks, such as the sound of a stream gurgling over rocks, or a steady breeze always blowing from the left. These are the kinds of landmarks you can use at night, too.

8 When you get back, take off your blindfold—sheesh, the daytime world is bright! Take this virtual night hike several times on different days. The more you practice, the easier *real* night walking will be.

night stalking

It's not your fault that you make noise when you walk. All humans are used to gallumping around on two big feet. But with practice you can learn to hush your feet and sneak quietly closer to wildlife (it's called stalking).

what you need

A place to walk

what to do

1 An area outdoors with a dirt or grassy surface is especially good for this but isn't absolutely necessary. You can practice night stalking anywhere, even in your own room.

2 Walk normally and notice how your legs and feet move. What part of your foot lands on the ground first? Then what happens? How far apart are your steps? Most people put their heel down first, then flop the rest of their foot forward. Humans usually take long steps, too. Clump, clump, clump.

3 Now try walking very quietly. How? If you're like most people, you'll try walking on your tiptoes. But what's the first thing that happens? You lose your balance and start to tip, so you stomp your other foot down to keep from falling. That's not a good way to be quiet!

4 Finally, try the stalk walk: Stand normally with your feet apart, but with one foot slightly ahead of the other. Keep your back, neck, and head straight and look forward like always, but bend your knees slightly so you're just barely crouching. Keep your arms at your sides and relax. (This stance is a lot like the one surfers and skateboarders use.)

5 Now slowly take a step forward with the foot that's farthest back. But keep your knees slightly bent as you move. And instead of planting your foot down heel first, put the outer side edge of your foot down first (see the photo, far right) and then slowly roll it to the inside until your whole foot is flat on the ground.

6 Use the same slow, smooth motion to take a short step with your other foot, and so on. Concentrate on taking short, easy steps.

7 When you practice this outdoors, notice each time you roll your foot from the outside to the inside whether you feel any sticks or stones that might make noise when you put your weight down. If you do, carefully move your foot to another spot and try again. Feel your way as you stalk-walk.

8 Keep practicing. At first this stalk walk will feel unnatural, but soon you'll be stalking with a smooth, easy motion—whisper quiet.

something else to try:
Put your stalking skills to the test by trying to sneak up on a chirping cricket or a calling frog. Both have super-sensitive hearing, so you'll have to be truly quiet. How close can you get before the cricket or frog hears you and suddenly stops making its night sounds?

how to sit still
(even when you don't feel like it)

Not every animal has great eyesight at night, but all animals are super-good at seeing one thing: movement. The tiniest out-of-the-ordinary motion is enough to send an animal running or a bird flying away. So one important key to getting a good, long look at wildlife—day or night—is to sit still and stay quiet.

Easier said than done! Humans (and maybe kids especially) have a hard time not moving. Go ahead and try it now: How long can you stay absolutely still, without moving your head, your arms, even your fingers? No fair scratching your head or shifting your weight from side to side! Ready . . . set . . . don't move! See? It doesn't take much sitting still before you get bored and restless. Something itches. Your neck's uncomfortable. You hear a noise but can't look without turning. Pretty soon . . . arggh! You've just got to move something. Experienced wildlife watchers have learned some tricks for sitting still. Try them, and you're sure to get a good look at more birds and animals.

1 Find a comfortable spot. You'll be sitting there a while, so make sure it's comfy. A soft, grassy place is good, or make a pile of dry leaves for a cushion. Just be sure there are no rocks, no prickly pinecones—and definitely no ant hills!

2 Sit down with your legs crossed under you and your arms and hands resting comfortably in your lap. If there's a tree behind you, use it as a backrest.

3 Now relax. Let your muscles and your body go limp. Stop thinking about stuff. Don't look for wildlife yet. Instead, stay still and think only about your breathing. Concentrate on the rhythm, the in and out of each easy, deep breath. In and out . . . in and out. Don't let thoughts of other things distract you; keep your mind strictly on your breathing. In and out . . . in and out . . . ahhh.

4 Relaxing like this for several minutes makes you less restless, more alert, and better able to cope with doing "nothing." Now you're ready to watch wildlife.

5 Stay still and don't turn your head. Just use your eyes to look around. You'll be surprised at how much you can see out of the sides of your eyes. If you start feeling restless, do some more easy breathing. Hey. . . isn't that a flying squirrel over there?

build a night exploring trail

Here's a way to give yourself a familiar place to explore at night, complete with ropes and glow-in-the-dark trail markers to guide you. You can use the trail to practice your night skills during the day, too.

what you need

A place in your yard to explore
  and watch wildlife
Work gloves
Garden shears or clippers (see Note)
Rope
Night blind (see page 22)
Glow-in-the-dark or white paint
Paintbrush
Rocks or concrete paving blocks
Plywood pieces,
  ¼ inch (6 mm) thick
Marker or pen
Acrylic paints
Small nails
Wooden stakes
Hammer

4 Make a rope "handrail" to guide you at night by tying rope along one side of the trail at about waist height. String the rope between trees and bushes, or drive long sticks into the ground every 3 or 4 feet (0.9 or 1.2 m) and tie the rope to them. At night, keep your flashlights off and follow the rope instead.

5 Make the night blind according to the instructions on page 22 and set it up to give you a great place for observing night creatures.

what to do

Note: Always ask a grownup for help using any kind of sharp tool, such as garden shears.

1 Figure out a good route for your trail. A wooded area that takes you by bushes or trees, where you can hide while you watch for wildlife, is especially good. But even a yard with an open lawn and just a few trees is fine, especially if you add a night blind for hiding (see page 22).

2 Once you've chosen the path, put on a pair of work gloves and remove any obstacles, such as rocks or fallen branches, that you might trip over or run into when you're walking on the trail after dark. With a grownup's help, use garden shears or clippers to snip away any branches growing into the path, too.

3 The path you've cleared for safety is all you really need for a night exploring trail. But you can also add other features such as the ones in the next steps.

6 Using a brush and glow-in-the-dark (or white) paint, paint designs on several rocks or concrete paving blocks to serve as trail markers. Then put the markers along one side of the trail (the side opposite the rope if you also used that). No way you'll get lost now!

7 Make night trail signs. Using a marking pen, draw designs such as a moon and stars, a raccoon, or an owl, on square or rectangular pieces of ¼-inch (6 mm) plywood. Outline the designs with glow-in-the-dark paint, then fill in the other areas with acrylic paint colors. To hang the signs, prop them up in or against trees or bushes, or attach them with nails to wooden stakes and drive the stakes into the ground.

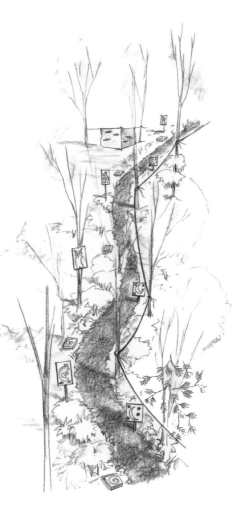

using your night trail

- Don't forget to look up. Many night creatures carry out their lives in the trees and sky above your head.

- Don't forget to look down. Ground beetles, earthworms, fireflies, and other interesting after-dark creatures might be right at your feet.

- Try watching for wildlife from different places along the trail. You'll be surprised at how each place gives you a slightly different view of the night world.

- Visit your night trail at different times of the night. What differences do you notice in the night's sights and sounds? Check out the positions of the Moon and stars from one time to the next. How much do they move in the sky in one hour, two hours, three?

night animals

At about the same time you're closing your eyes to go to sleep, night animals are opening theirs and waking up. It's their turn to get busy finding food and raising families.

Bats zip through the skies gobbling insects. Raccoons climb trees and swim streams. Opossums waddle across lawns. Deer and foxes roam open fields. Frogs and toads sing. Mice and salamanders skitter among fallen leaves.

An amazing number of animals are *nocturnal,* or active at night. On the next few pages, you'll discover fun facts about some common after-dark animals. But the most fun of all is staying up late and seeing them for yourself! How many do you think you might see when you go night exploring?

the after-dark gang

Shhhh . . . something's out there! In fact, you'll probably find a *lot* of things out there in the darkness, once you start really looking at nighttime nature.

OPOSSUMS

With a long naked tail, pink pointed nose, beady eyes, and scruffy long-haired body, an opossum looks like it's part rat, part cat—and part alien from another planet. In a way, it *is* from a different world, or at least a different time. The opossum is the oldest living mammal in North America. Its ancestors were waddling around dinosaur backyards 100 million years ago.

The opossum is also North America's only *marsupial.* Most marsupials, such as kangaroos and koalas, live in Australia. Marsupials give birth to tiny young that crawl into their mother's pouch to nurse for the first months of their lives. When opossum babies move to their mom's pouch, they're the size of navy beans. After two to three months, they've grown enough to climb out and cling to mom's furry back as she hunts for food at night.

Opossums have *prehensile* tails. That means they can use their tails to grab onto branches, like monkeys can. Their hind feet are prehensile, too. Using its tail and hind feet, an opossum can climb trees and scurry through branches.

Have you heard of "playing possum"? When attacked by a predator, an opossum really will roll over and seem dead, with its tongue hanging out and its body limp and still. It's a good trick, because most predators eat only living prey. Dead 'possum? Uck—and they walk away. But a conked-out opossum isn't playing dead. It really is *out*—

Hitching a ride: When they're old enough to leave their mother's pouch, baby opossums climb aboard her back, hang onto her long fur, and go wherever she goes.

so scared it just keeled over. Sometimes it takes more than an hour for the petrified opossum to "wake up."

Opossums are known as "walking garbage cans" because they eat almost anything they can find, including insects, frogs, snakes, other animals (even dead ones), worms, birds, berries, and garbage.

WHERE TO LOOK FOR OPOSSUMS:
Anyplace there's food! Keep an eye out for opossums visiting garbage cans, vegetable gardens, and berry bushes.

Beady eyes, jagged teeth, scraggly fur, pink-skinned feet . . . no wonder this opossum is grinning. It must look funny even to itself!

a 21-bean brain?

Opossums are tough, but they're not especially smart. In fact, they're animals of very little brain. In one study, a scientist could fit only 21 beans into the brain space of an opossum skull but needed 150 beans to fill a raccoon's.

bean brain experiment

opossum brain=21 beans

raccoon brain=150 beans

Jump!

FLYING SQUIRRELS

A flying squirrel can't really fly, but it sure knows how to get around at night: The squirrel flings itself from a branch and free-falls long enough to gather speed (photo, above), then spreads all four legs and opens its four-cornered "parachute," a layer of skin stretching across its belly and connecting wrist to ankle on each side (photo, right). Gliding, it uses its flat tail as a rudder to steer toward its target, usually a tree trunk. Then it raises its forepaws and the front of the chute to slow down, and lands with a *click* of grasping claws. From there the squirrel scampers to the ground to dig for food or climbs up the tree to jump again to another tree.

Not all flying squirrels are little. The red giant flying squirrel of Asia is almost 3 feet (0.9 m) long! The two kinds that live in North America are much smaller. The northern flying squirrel is about 11 inches (27.5 cm) long, and the southern flying squirrel is only about 8 inches (20 cm). Both kinds spend their nights jumping and gliding from tree to tree searching for nuts,

seeds, berries, moths, tree sap, and mushrooms. Gliding is faster and easier than walking when you're a little squirrel with short legs.

In late summer, flying squirrels start storing nuts for the winter by poking them into the ground or in holes or cracks in trees. One squirrel can hide as many as 15,000 nuts. Another way flying squirrels survive cold winters is by snuggling up with other flying squirrels. Sometimes a dozen or more squirrels share the same winter den.

Navigating at night is no problem for the flying squirrel. Its big, bulging dark eyes are made for night

Glide!

vision. It also has long, sensitive whiskers called *vibrissae* for feeling its way around. And it uses special scent glands on its cheeks to mark its path so that it can follow its nose to important takeoff and landing spots.

WHERE TO LOOK FOR FLYING SQUIRRELS:

Up! Unfortunately, flying squirrels are small and quiet and hard to see in trees after dark. You might hear them, though. Listen for soft, bird-like chirping sounds. Usually, birds don't chirp at night. But flying squirrels do.

41

Fat and happy, this raccoon has found one of its favorite munchies: wild grapes.

RACCOONS

You have a good chance of seeing a raccoon at night. They're found almost everywhere, in towns and cities as well as forests, in the United States, Mexico, and parts of Canada. Raccoons have "masked bandit" faces and bushy black-and-white ringed tails. An adult can weigh up to 40 pounds (18.2 kg)—as much as an average-size dog.

Raccoons are *omnivorous*. In other words, they eat all kinds of foods. In the woods they eat berries, nuts, grapes, worms, insects, frogs, crayfish, turtles, and small animals such as mice. Raccoons that live closer to people also raid garbage pails and dumpsters for food we throw away. They especially like sweets and fast food (does that sound like anyone you know?).

Raccoons prefer to live near water and are good swimmers. They're also great climbers. Their forepaws have long, flexible fingers and a thumb, like small human hands. A raccoon can use its forepaws to open clams or grab an egg from a nest. It can even turn doorknobs and open pop-top cans!

People used to think that raccoons wash their food by dipping it in water. Today scientists know that raccoons only dunk food they find near water, and aren't really washing it. They're probably just feeling the food to make sure it's good before taking a bite.

In spring, mother raccoons give birth to between four and seven babies. A newborn raccoon is blind, hairless, and about the size of a chicken egg. It'll fit in the palm of your hand. Within a couple of months young raccoons are wide-eyed and furry and ready to follow their mother into the night. If you listen carefully in spring and early summer, you might hear a mother raccoon chattering and purring at her babies to keep them near her.

WHERE TO LOOK FOR RACCOONS:

Use a flashlight to search for raccoons along streamsides and the edges of ponds, near garbage pails, and in trees with wild grapevines. If two small, yellow eyes glow back at you, you've probably found a "back-yard bandit."

STRIPED SKUNKS

Crash! You hear a banging noise in your yard and run outside. Something knocked over a garbage can. Let's see . . . it's black, about the size of a cat, with a fluffy tail and—yikes—white stripes on its head, back, and tail! Skunk! Time to run back in the house!

Actually, unless the skunk is too close or acting scared, you can probably take time for another look. Watching skunks, like watching any wildlife, is fun and safe as long as you stay still and quiet and keep your distance—with skunks, at least 40 feet (36 m). Always follow the Rules for Watching Wildlife on page 49.

Striped skunks are among the most common mammals in North America. They're in every state in the United States, plus Canada and Mexico. Skunks can dig burrows but don't usually bother. Instead they move into another animal's hole, or in drainage pipes, beneath buildings, or in wood or rock piles. Their favorite foods are insects, grubs, worms—and garbage if they can get it.

The stinky stuff skunks spray is called musk. It's stored in two berry-size glands below the skunk's tail. Other animals such as minks produce musk, but it's not as smelly. And only skunks can aim and spray their musk. They can squirt it 15 feet (13.5 m) or more and hit their target every time. It's so strong it can blind you temporarily or make you vomit. Even other skunks hate skunk spray.

Skunks don't spray unless an enemy is too close or frightens them. Their black-and-white fur is a warning: watch out! If an animal or person doesn't take the hint, the skunk will arch its back, raise its tail, and stamp its front feet. That's the final warning: get out fast! If that doesn't work, the skunk turns its rear around so both its head and rump are facing the target, and sprays—*peeyew!*

WHERE TO LOOK FOR SKUNKS:

Strictly from a distance! Skunks rarely spray humans, but don't take the chance. During the day, look for clawed-up holes and dirt in your lawn. They're signs a skunk may have been digging there for food.

Warning! There's no mistaking this skunk's message: You'd better turn tail and leave before it turns its tail and sprays.

these skunk jokes stink!

Q: What kind of books do skunks read?
A: Best smellers!

Q: Why are skunks always arguing?
A: Because they like to raise a stink!

Q: How many skunks does it take to make a big stink?
A: Quite a phew!

hide and survive:
play the night animal game

Nocturnal animals are really good hiders. That's why you have to look and listen so carefully to spot them. Can you hide like a night animal? Can you spot your "night animal" friends? Play this game of night-time hide-and-seek to find out.

what you need
3 or 4 friends
A path or trail in a park or yard
   with trees and bushes

what to do
Note: Start playing this game around sunset, when there's still enough light to see but not as much as during the day. How does the game change after the sun goes down? What is easier and what is harder?

1 Choose one person to be the "night animal." While the others look away and count slowly to 60, the night animal finds a good hiding spot along the path or trail. The animal can't go more than 3 feet (0.9 m) off the trail. (Some hints: Animals use leaves and bushes as "cover" to hide behind. And they stay low to the ground or press themselves close against a tree trunk or branch to make their bodies less noticeable.)

2 When the others are done counting they walk quietly down the path or trail looking for the animal. No fair leaving the path. You have to stay on it! Remember to listen as well as look for the animal.

3 If the others walk past the animal without seeing or hearing it, the animal wins.

something else to try:
After you've played this game several times, think about why some kids were easy to find and others weren't. Did the color of their clothes have something to do with it? As the night became darker, was color as important? Imagine yourself as a real night animal trying to hide from a predator.

DEER MICE

House mice are dark gray with almost-naked tails. Maybe you've even seen one living in your home. But not all mice are house mice. Most kinds live outdoors and play important roles in nature. And most are active—you guessed it, at night.

Of the more than 250 different kinds of mice in North America, the most common are the white-footed mouse and its near twin, the deer mouse. Even scientists have a hard time telling them apart and sometimes just lump them together as "deer mice." Both are way cuter than your average gray house mouse, with big black eyes, rusty-brown fur on top, and white fur on their feet and bellies.

White-footed and deer mice live in woods and meadows where there are plenty of nuts, seeds, small insects, and berries. They hunt for food on the ground and in shrubs and trees, using their long tails for balance when climbing. Scientists don't know why, but white-footed mice often drum their feet on grass or a leaf to make a buzzing sound. When eating, they sometimes purr softly.

Tiptoes and a tail are enough for this white-footed mouse to balance between two spindly grapevines. (Yum! Wild raisins!)

White-footed and deer mice build small rounded nests made of dry grass. They nest in small burrows, hollow logs, and woodpiles. A single white-footed mouse mother can have as many as eight litters and 50 babies a year. When they're only six weeks old, "baby" mice can reproduce, too. So why aren't we up to our ears in mice? Because they're an important food for many birds and animals. Without lots of mice and voles to eat, hawks, foxes, owls, and many other meat eaters would starve.

WHERE TO LOOK FOR WHITE-FOOTED AND DEER MICE:

At night, listen for tiny drumming, chirping, or rustling noises in fallen leaves and low bushes. Then look carefully in the direction of the sound. You might catch a glimpse of the mouse before it scampers into a hiding place.

COTTONTAIL RABBITS

Have you ever seen a rabbit dance? On clear spring nights, groups of male and female cottontail rabbits "dance" beneath the Moon to choose mates. If you sit quietly at the edge of a park or field where you know rabbits live, you might get to watch. The cottontails run and jump high into the air, playing leapfrog over each other, kicking at the starry sky, sometimes doing backward flips. Suddenly they'll rush into the bushes as though playing hide-and-seek, then burst out onto the field again, racing and kicking some more. When a female is interested in a male, she shows him by jumping up and punching him with her forefeet!

Several kinds of cottontail rabbits live in North America. The eastern cottontail is the most common. It weighs between 3 and 4 pounds (1.4 and 1.8 kg) and has 3-inch-long (7.6 cm), super-sensitive ears that it can rotate to hear from the front, back, and sides. In the winter it nibbles at twigs and bark. In spring and summer, it eats green plants. All cottontails love to eat garden vegetables!

Of course, cottontails are named for their round fuzzy tails, which look like cotton balls. The rabbits flash their tails when they run. Cottontails also thump their feet on the ground to warn other rabbits when danger is near. If it can't escape an enemy, a cottontail fights fiercely, using its strong legs and sharp teeth and claws.

A female cottontail rabbit makes her nest by digging out a shallow, bowl-like area on the ground and lining it with grass, dry leaves, and fur from her belly. Then she uses more grass to make a "blanket" to pull over the top of the nest. In one year, a mother cottontail rabbit may have as many as seven litters of four to five babies each. That's a bunch of bunnies!

WHERE TO LOOK FOR COTTONTAIL RABBITS:

Watch for rabbits nibbling grass in lawns, meadows, and parks just before and after sunset.

This baby cottontail rabbit probably has lots of brothers and sisters. Mother cottontails can have 30 or more babies a year.

American toad

FROGS AND TOADS

Ching-ching-ching-ching. Jug-a-rum, brrrr-wum. Cheeeeeeeeee. Chirrup, chirrup. All spring and summer, frogs and toads come out at night and fill the darkness with their songs. Actually, the songs are mating calls. Only male frogs and toads make them, to attract females and to tell other males to stay out of their territory.

How do frogs and toads make such big sounds? Even the tiny spring peeper, a frog about the size of your thumbnail, can be heard for more than half a mile.

A frog or toad breathes air into its lungs, then closes its mouth and nostrils and pumps the air back and forth across its vocal chords, which vibrate and make sound. On the "out" breath, the air fills the creature's vocal sac, blowing it up like a balloon. On the "in" breath, the sac collapses, forcing the air back across the vocal chords and into the lungs again. Over and over again, air pumps across the vocal chords. Over and over again, a mating call goes out. In a single night, a male frog or toad may call thousands, or even tens of thousands, of times.

Like most *amphibians,* frogs and toads are born with gills and spend the first part of their lives in water. Then they lose their gills, grow lungs and legs, and live on land as adults. Tadpoles swimming in a pond are baby frogs or toads, hatched from gooey masses of eggs laid there by females. It takes two years for a bullfrog tadpole to become an adult. Other kinds grow up in just a few weeks.

WHERE TO LOOK FOR FROGS AND TOADS:

Look for frogs at the edges of ponds and streams. Toads like moist, shady places. Look beneath bushes and in flower and vegetable gardens.

Mouthful of music: This tree frog is singing for a mate by puffing air in and out, back and forth across its vocal chords.

47

jump *how far?*

Stand in one place and jump forward as far as you can. How far did you jump compared to how tall you are? Some frogs can jump 20 times the length of their bodies. If you're 5 feet (1.5 m) tall and could do that, you could jump 100 feet (30.5 m), more than three times the world record!

Sproing! Frogs such as this green tree frog can leap really long distances. Powerful back legs spring them forward and stocky front legs soften their landing.

Some night creatures are so secretive that you might never see them. Spotted salamanders spend their lives beneath logs or in underground tunnels. They come out only for a few nights each spring to mate.

OTHER NIGHT ANIMALS

The animals you've read about so far are only a few of the more common members of the after-dark gang. Many other animals also are nocturnal. Some, such as beavers (which live in water) and armadillos (which need warm, dry land), can live only in certain kinds of places, or habitats. Others, such as foxes, deer, and elk, need lots of territory or certain types of foods. What special kinds of night animals live in your area? Keep a list of all the nocturnal creatures you see.

rules for watching wildlife

Wild animals aren't like pets or animals in a zoo. They're constantly struggling to survive. If you're not careful, you can hurt them without even knowing it. They could hurt you by mistake, too. Always follow these rules when watching animals in nature.

- *Keep your distance.* Leave plenty of room between you and wildlife. That way, you can both feel safe. If you want a closer look, use binoculars.

- *Don't scare or chase birds or animals.* Living in nature is hard. Wild creatures need all the energy they have just to survive. Don't make them run or fly unnecessarily.

- *Never, ever catch or touch a wild animal*—not even a cute little baby! Many creatures in the wild have insect pests, such as fleas, or diseases that can be dangerous to you if you get bitten. And most wild animals *will* bite if you try to touch or hold them. That's not because they're mean. It's just their instinct, one that helps them survive.

footprints in the night

Tracks and sign: The deer's footprint is an obvious track, but there's sign here, too. That lumpy pile of dirt is worm sign, castings left by an earthworm. The leaves, pine needles, and acorn are sign, too, from the trees that dropped them.

What kinds of birds and animals are moving around in your yard at night while you're asleep? One way to find out is to study the footprints, or *tracks,* they leave behind. Besides footprints, night creatures also leave other telltale traces of their comings and goings, such as fur, feathers, gnawed twigs, and droppings. Trackers call this kind of evidence *sign.* Studying tracks and sign is a great way to get a peek at the private lives of your nature neighbors.

How do you "read" tracks and sign and the stories they tell? Experts spend years learning the fine points. Really good trackers can read tracks on plain rock! But you don't have to be an expert. Some tracks and sign are easy to figure out. Look at the clues in the chart below. See? Sometimes "tracking" is just a matter of thinking like a detective.

Of course, learning to recognize the different shapes of tracks left by different animals helps you to read them, just like learning the shapes of letters helped you to read words. On the next few pages you'll find some fun ways to practice recognizing tracks.

tracks	where found	sign	the story
Small, hand-shaped tracks	In soft dirt around garbage pail	Garbage pail tipped over and pieces of trash scattered about	An opossum or raccoon got into your garbage.
Long, narrow, wet footprints with five rounded toes each	On bathroom floor	Damp, crumpled towel. Steam on mirror.	You just took a shower!

make a track station

Tracks are easiest to see in soft surfaces such as mud or loose dirt. That's why stream banks and garden beds are good places to look for tracks. Or, you can make your own good place, and then make sure animals walk there by attracting them with bait. Wildlife biologists call these places track stations.

what you need

Piece of plywood board, about 3 x 3 feet (91.4 x 91.4 cm)
Flour, cornmeal, sand, or soft dirt
Empty tuna can or small block of wood
Spoon
Peanut butter

what to do

1 Just before sunset, find a level spot that's in the open but near tall grass, trees, or shrubs (at the edge of a lawn, for example). Put the board flat on the ground and sprinkle flour, cornmeal, sand, or soft dirt over its entire surface. Make sure the edges are covered, too. The layer should be ¼ to ½ inch (6 to 13 mm) deep. Smooth it with your hands so it's even. Then put the can or block of wood in the middle of the board and spoon a glob of peanut butter on top.

2 Come back the next morning to check for footprints on your track station. How many different kinds of tracks are there? Use a field guide to help you figure out what birds or animals made them. To "reset" your track station, just smooth out the layer of material.

something else to try:

Do different baits attract different kinds of creatures? Besides peanut butter, try birdseed, cereal, berries, or other foods.

walk like a fox, waddle like an opossum

Animals have different ways of walking that make different patterns on the ground. So even if the footprints they leave behind are hard to recognize, the patterns, or how the tracks are arranged, can tell you what kind of creature was probably there.

A good way to learn the patterns is to imitate how some animals move. Get down on all fours and pretend that your hands are front feet and your knees are rear feet (use your own feet as rear feet for the weasel and rabbit patterns).

Ready? Okay, walk like a . . .

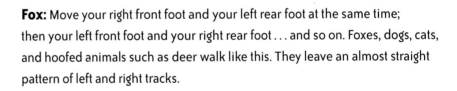

Fox: Move your right front foot and your left rear foot at the same time; then your left front foot and your right rear foot . . . and so on. Foxes, dogs, cats, and hoofed animals such as deer walk like this. They leave an almost straight pattern of left and right tracks.

Opossum: Move your left front and left rear feet at the same time, then your right front and right rear feet, and so on. Notice how you sort of waddle from one side to the other? Opossums, bears, raccoons, and beavers all walk this way and leave a zigzag pattern of front and rear tracks.

Weasel: This walking style is more like hopping. Reach out and move both your front feet as far forward as you can, then bring your rear feet up just behind the front. Weasels and other animals that move this way are called bounders and leave a boxy, side-by-side pattern.

Rabbit: You won't be able to do this one without falling over, but it's fun to try. Reach forward with both front feet just as you did for the weasel walk, but then bring your rear feet *in front of* and to either side of your forefeet, and try to push off again with those rear feet. Rabbits, squirrels, and most mice walk this way (but humans sure can't!). They leave a diamond-shaped pattern.

track casting

The footprints you find today don't have to disappear with the next rain. Here's how to keep a record of the tracks you find by making casts of them from plaster. Over time your collection of cast tracks will reveal the life stories of the animals in your yard.

what you need
Animal track
Sponge
Empty cardboard milk or juice container
Scissors
Quick-drying plaster of Paris
Spoon
Water
Petroleum jelly or vegetable oil
Trowel
Pie pan or cookie sheet

what to do

1 Clear any leaves, stones, or sticks from around and inside the track. If water has puddled inside the track, use the sponge to soak it up so the track is dry.

2 With scissors cut the top off the cardboard container. Then cut a strip 2 to 3 inches (5 to 7.5 cm) wide from the part remaining, to make a small square enclosure for the track. Spread petroleum jelly or vegetable oil on the square's inside surface. Then carefully place the "fence" around the track (see the photo, top right).

3 If there are any gaps between the cardboard strip and the ground, sprinkle dirt around the outside to fill them. The cardboard will keep the plaster of Paris from spreading out in a big puddle.

4 Use the bottom of the container for mixing the Plaster of Paris. Pour enough plaster into the container to fill the track, plus a little more. Stir constantly as you add just enough water to make the mixture thick and creamy—like pudding.

5 Pour the plaster of Paris mixture into the track and square until it's about 1 inch (2.5 cm) deep.

6 Let the cast sit for 30 minutes, until the plaster of Paris firms up. Use the trowel to carefully dig around and under the track, keeping the cardboard in place, to loosen the cast from the soil. Don't touch the cast yet because the plaster won't be fully dry. Use the trowel to slide the cast (with the square) onto the cookie sheet and carry it indoors to harden overnight.

7 In the morning, remove the cardboard from the cast and brush the dirt off the track with your fingers or an old toothbrush. Can you tell what kind of track it is? Use a field guide to help you identify it. Write the name of the animal on the bottom of the cast. Now find more tracks to add to your collection.

something else to try:

- Photograph the tracks you find. Take close-up shots—but don't use a flash. Too much light in a photo washes out a footprint's details.
- Collect whole tracks. If you find a track in soft mud, cut a square around the outside of the track with an old table knife, then use a spatula to scoop beneath the track and lift it out. Put the track "brick" on a board or cookie sheet to study.

tracks you might find

raccoon

gray squirrel

white-footed mouse

white-tailed deer

bats, bats, bats!

Flying fur! This little brown bat's fingered wings let it dive, swerve, soar, and scoop up bugs. If you look carefully you can see its hooked thumbs, one on each wing.

They're blind. They suck your blood. They make nests in your hair. They're . . . totally untrue myths about bats! Here's the *real* story.

THEY'RE EVERYWHERE

Tigers, humans, cats, goats, whales, dogs, pigs, giraffes, mice, cows—they're all different kinds of mammals. But did you know that one out of every four kinds of mammal in the world can *fly?* It's true—because about one-fourth of all the world's mammals are *bats.* Bats are the only animals that can truly fly ("flying" squirrels only glide).

There are nearly 1,000 different kinds of bats. Most live in Asia, Central America, South America, and other tropical places where temperatures are always warm and food is always plentiful. But bats also live almost everywhere else in the world. No matter where you are, bats are almost surely living near you. There are 43 different kinds of bats in the United States, and about 37 kinds in Europe.

GENTLE DEBUGGERS

Some of the bats that live in deserts and rain forests sip nectar from night-blooming flowers and are important pollinators. Without them, people would have a hard time growing crops such as bananas, dates, cashews, and mangoes. Several kinds of tropical bats swoop down over water and catch frogs or fish for dinner. Only three kinds of bats, called vampire bats, bite birds or animals (almost never humans) and suck small amounts of blood. Vampire bats live only in Latin America.

The bats hanging out in your neighborhood are shy, gentle creatures that eat insects—*lots* of insects. Bats are the world's champion bug hunters. Scientists say that bats eat about half their body weight in insects each night. If you ate that much and weigh 80 pounds (36.3 kg), you'd gobble down 40 pounds (18.2 kg) of food for supper. Burp! That's a big burger!

It's a good thing we have bats for neighbors, or we'd be spending all our time swatting at mosquitoes and other flying bugs.

Bat Wings Are Built Like Hands

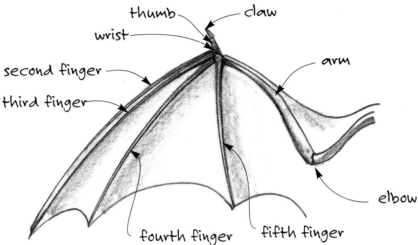

thumb · claw · wrist · second finger · third finger · arm · elbow · fourth finger · fifth finger

WINGS WITH FINGERS

Like birds, bats have wings that are supported by arm bones. But bats also have finger bones and a thumb built into each wing. The thumbs have a little hook at the end for clinging to tree branches or cave walls. The fingers are webbed together with a double layer of skin that covers the wings and connects to the bat's body. A bat's fingers are really long compared to its body. If your fingers were as big, they'd be longer than your legs.

If you ate as much as a bat, you'd have to swallow half your weight in food every night.

FLEXIBLE FLIERS

Because of their finger bones, bat wings are almost like hands. A bat can make a scoop out of its wings to catch insects in the air and pop them into its mouth. To fly, a bat doesn't flap its wings up and down like a bird. Instead, it "swims" through the air. It reaches forward with its webbed wings, grabs some air, and pulls its body ahead while using its legs to kick backward.

The bat's flexible wings give it amazing maneuverability, like a living stunt plane. By folding its wings into different shapes, the bat can change direction quickly, zooming and tumbling through the air. It can

Bat Echolocation

A bat finds food at night by sending out sound waves and following the echoes that bounce back off insects.

roll, climb, dive, somersault, zip one way, then screech to a hover, all in an instant. If you're an insect and a bat is chasing you—yikes! You're in trouble!

HEARING IS SEEING

How do bats find tiny flying insects in the dark? Bats aren't blind, but even good eyesight isn't enough help. Bats use sound, or *echolocation*, to help find their way around and locate prey at night.

Have you ever shouted in a big, empty room and heard your voice come back to you as an echo? The sound waves you made when you shouted bounced off a wall and traveled back to your ears. A bat sends out high-pitched squeaks and clicks almost constantly. The sounds are *ultrasonic*, which means their pitch is too high for humans to hear. But the sounds behave the same way your shout did. They come bouncing back to the bat.

A bat can tell from the echoes bouncing back to it how close an object is, what size and shape it is, and whether it's moving. A bat can detect an object as small as a human hair. It can "hear" a twig or branch in time to avoid flying into it. It can tell insects it likes to eat from those it doesn't. In a flock of hundreds of bats, each bat recognizes and reacts to the echoes of its own special sounds.

What gives bats this amazing ability to see by hearing? Scientists aren't exactly sure. But part of the answer is in the features that make most bats so strange looking: their odd-shaped ears and nose. The ears of most bats have folds of skin and a cone-shaped growth, called a *tragus*, that help the bat tell whether an echo is coming from high or low, left or right. And researchers think that at least some bats use their snouts to "aim" high-pitched clicks at an insect. When a bat is searching for a meal, it sends out about 10 clicks per second. When it detects an insect, it speeds up its clicks to almost 200 per second and focuses them on the target. The closer the bat gets to the bug, the faster its echoes bounce back, until—chomp—no more echoes, no more bug.

where are the bats in your neighborhood?

Bats spend the daylight hours in safe, out-of-the-way places such as caves, attics, or hollow trees. This big brown bat is roosting in an old woodpecker hole.

Most bats spend the day roosting, or sleeping, hanging upside down in out-of-the-way places protected from the weather. Some kinds live in groups in caves, under bridges, or in empty parts of buildings (such as an attic). Other kinds live alone in hollow trees or hang from branches. Sometimes a bat will find a perch behind a window shutter or beneath a porch ceiling. Bats are shy and secretive, so if you see one roosting you're really lucky! Take a good look, but don't touch the bat or bother it.

play catch with a bat

Bats use ultrasound to find insects in the night sky. Their loud clicks are too high-pitched for us to hear them. But here's a way to watch a bat's bug detector in action.

what you need

Yard or other open area
1 or more bats flying at dusk
Small pebbles

what to do

1 When a bat is flying overhead, toss a pebble into the air near it (but not *at* it). The bat will instantly detect and dive toward the pebble, aiming its sound waves at the object. When the echoes coming back don't say "bug," the bat will turn away and start searching again for the real thing.

2 Try throwing pebbles different distances from the bat. How far away can the bat detect a pebble?

something else to try:
Watch bats chasing moths near streetlights (of course, you need to be careful, and don't stand *in* the street). Bright streetlights attract lots of insects at night, and bats have learned to hunt there for easy meals.

build a bat house

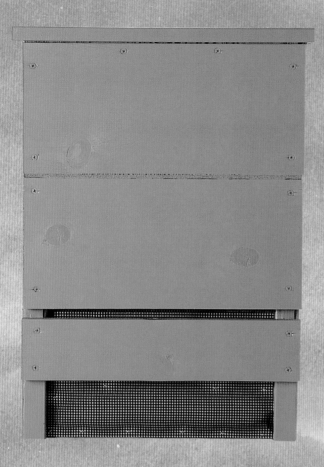

what you need

A grownup to help you (see Note), plus:

MATERIALS AND SUPPLIES

1 X 8 pine shelving board, 8 feet long
  (2.4 m) (see Note 2)
1 X 4 pine shelving board, 3 feet long
  (0.9 m) (see Note 2)
Medium-grit sandpaper
1 X 2 pine furring strip (see Note 2)
Roll, at least 15 feet long (4.5 m),
  of ¾-inch-wide (1.9 cm),
  ³⁄₁₆-inch-thick (5 mm)
  self-adhesive waterproof
  weather-stripping tape
13 x 22-inch (33 x 55.9 cm) piece
  of plastic needlepoint netting
  (available at craft stores) or fiber
  glass (not metal) window screen
30 1⅝-inch (4.1 cm) galvanized
  outdoor decking screws
Metal hanging brackets with screws
Exterior latex paint, brown

TOOLS

Tape measure
Ruler or carpenter's square
Pencil
Handsaw or power saw
Heavy-duty staple gun with ⅜-
  or ½-inch (9.5 or 13 mm) staples
Hammer
Screwdriver or power drill with
  screwdriver bit (recommended)
Scissors and knife
Paintbrush

Bats are great insect hunters. Just one little brown bat can eat 600 mosquitoes in an hour. Bats gobble up garden pests, too. Plus, they're fun to watch. Unfortunately, many kinds of bats are endangered because humans have disturbed or destroyed their natural homes. This simple bat house requires only a few tools and will give some of the bats in your neighborhood a safe home.

Cutting Diagram

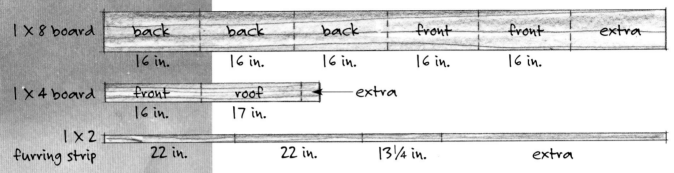

1 X 8 board	back	back	back	front	front	extra
	16 in.	16 in.	16 in.	16 in.	16 in.	

1 X 4 board	front	roof	← extra
	16 in.	17 in.	

1 X 2 furring strip	22 in.	22 in.	13¼ in.	extra

Note: To convert to metrics, multiply the measurement in inches by 2.54 to determine centimeters or by 25.40 for millimeters.

what to do

Note: You'll need a grownup to help you choose and measure the materials for your bat house and also to help with the sawing, drilling, and other steps that require power tools. Your helper will come in handy for holding parts while you screw them together, too.

Note 2: The actual dimensions of a 1 X 8 board are ¾ x 7½ inches (1.9 x 19 cm). The actual dimensions of a 1 X 4 board are ¾ x 3½ inches (1.9 x 8.9 cm). The actual dimensions of a 1 X 2 furring strip are ¾ x 1½ inches (1.9 x 3.8 cm).

1 Using the tape measure, ruler or square, and a pencil, measure and mark the cut lines for the bat house parts on the two pine shelving boards, as shown above.

2 Use the saw to cut the pieces you've marked. Lightly write each part's name (back, front, roof) on the pieces as you cut them, to help you keep track of them. You should have three back pieces, three front pieces (one narrower than the others), and one roof. Sand the cut edges of all the pieces to smooth them.

3 Now measure, mark, and cut the pine furring strip into three pieces, two measuring 22 inches

(55.9 cm) long and one 13¼ inches (33.7 cm) long. These pieces form the house's inside frame between the front and back boards.

4 Place the three back boards on a hard, flat surface, lined up one above the other just as they'll be when you put them together (see the drawing on page 62). Apply a strip of weather-stripping tape along the top and bottom edges of the middle back board. Then push the three boards together to form the back of the house.

5 With your helper holding the back boards firmly together, so the foam weather-stripping between them is compressed, staple the plastic netting or window screen over the

Bat House (Exploded View)

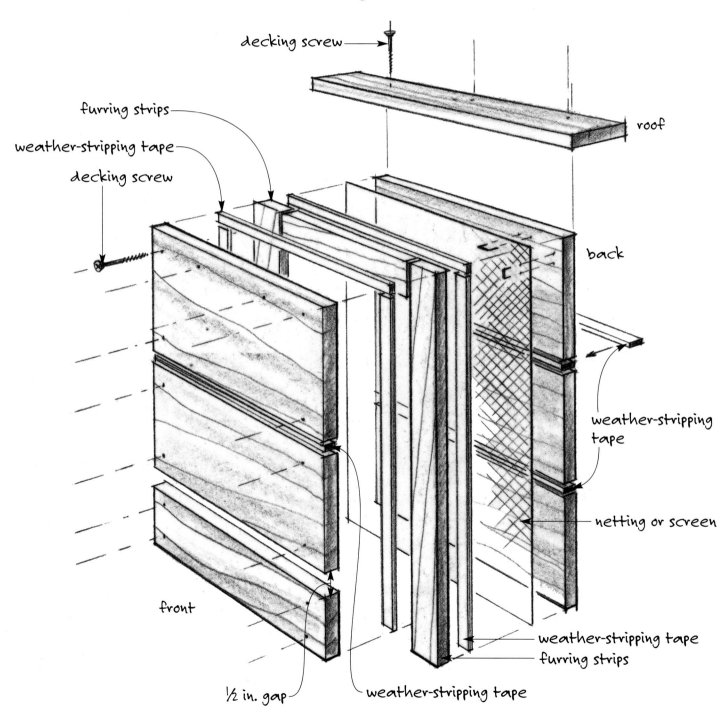

decking screw

furring strips

weather-stripping tape

decking screw

roof

back

weather-stripping tape

netting or screen

weather-stripping tape

furring strips

front

½ in. gap

weather-stripping tape

three back boards. Be sure the netting extends all the way to the bottom edge of the lowest board. The netting should be tight, with no puckers or bends. If any staples stick out, hammer them flush to the boards.

6 Now you're ready to work on the inside frame. Apply weather-stripping tape down the full length of both sides of all three pieces of pine furring. Now position the pine furring strips over the netting, with the two longest pieces on the left and right sides of the back boards and the short one across the top (see the drawing).

7 Position one of the two widest front boards over the furring strips, level with the top, as shown in the drawing. Attach it to the frame with two screws on each side.

8 Apply weather-stripping tape along one long edge of the other wide front board. Position the board on the frame with the weather-stripping tape pushed against the bottom edge of the top front board, and screw it to the frame, again using two screws on each side.

9 Now screw the 1 x 4 front board to the frame, but leave a ½-inch (1.3 cm) ventilation gap between it and the other two front boards (see the drawing, left, and photo on page 60).

10 Use a knife to trim and peel away the weather-stripping tape exposed on the inside frame between and below the front boards. Congratulations! You've finished the front of the house.

11 Now turn the house over and screw the back panels in place to the frame, much as you did the front panels (but without leaving a ventilation gap).

12 Position the roof board so that its back edge is flush along the house's back edge and extends evenly over both sides and the front. Before attaching it, apply weather-stripping tape along the house's top to seal the cracks between the upper front and back boards and the inside frame. Then push the roof down in place over the tape and drive screws through the top down into the frame to attach it.

13 Screw metal hanging brackets to the top back.

14 Hooray, you've just built a bat house! Paint it with exterior latex house paint to protect the wood. In most climates you should use a dark color, such as brown or black, to absorb heat and help keep the bats in your house warm at night. If you live in a dry, desertlike area, paint it a lighter color to help keep it cooler.

15 Hang your bat house at least 10 feet (3 m) up on the side of a house or other building (trees aren't good places because they're too shady). The bat house should face east or south to get as much sun as possible.

bats you might see

Little Brown Bat

Big Brown Bat

American state, including Hawaii, and also in Canada and Latin America. The ones that live where winters get cold migrate south in fall. A hoary bat's wings are 16 inches (40.6 cm) across—about as long as your arm from wrist to shoulder.

MEXICAN FREE-TAILED BAT

This little bat is called "free tailed" because about 2 inches (5 cm) of its tail stick out behind its rear membrane. Mexican free-tailed bats live in groups in buildings and caves. Over 20 million live in the world's largest bat colony, in Bracken Cave, Texas. In summer they fill the skies, eating about 250 tons (226.8 t) of insects every night.

Different kinds of bats live in different parts of the world. If you live in North America, you might see one of these common kinds.

LITTLE BROWN BAT

At only 3 to 4 inches (7.6 to 10 cm) long and weighing only ¼ to ⅓ ounce (7 to 10 g), this bat really is little. Its appetite is huge, though. Little brown bats especially like to live near a marsh or lake where there are lots of mosquitoes and other insects to eat.

BIG BROWN BAT

These bats often hang out with little brown bats, and roost alone or in groups in buildings, beneath roof overhangs, or sometimes in hollow trees. They eat all sorts of

insects but like beetles especially. A big brown bat has long, dark brown fur. Its wingspan measures 1 foot (30 cm) across.

HOARY BAT

These bats have white-tipped fur ("hoary" means "frosted") and roost alone in trees. They live in every

Hoary Bat

Mexican Free-tailed Bat

be a bat (moth!)
play bat and moth

What's it like for a bat to use sound instead of sight to catch a moth? In this game, called Bat and Moth, you and your friends will have fun taking turns to find out.

what you need
4 or more friends
   (grownups can play, too)
Blindfolds
A yard or other large, open area

what to do

1 Decide who will be the "bat" and who will be the "moth" first (you'll play this game more than once and take turns, so everybody will get a chance). Everyone else is a "tree."

2 Blindfold the bat. Don't leave any places to peek through!

3 All the trees stand forming a big circle, with the bat and the moth in the center of the circle.

4 The object of the game is for the bat to catch and touch the moth while the moth tries to escape. Both the bat and the moth can move around inside the circle of trees but can't go outside it.

5 To start, spin the bat around three times. Then the bat shouts "bat!" and the moth must immediately say "moth!" back. The game begins! The bat moves in the direction of the sound to catch the moth while the moth tries to stay away. The bat can call "bat!" again and again, as many times as it wants, and every time the moth must instantly answer "moth!" If the bat or

moth bumps into one of the trees, that tree shouts "tree!"

6 The game ends when the bat touches the moth (or when you're all laughing too hard to keep playing!). The moth gets to be the bat for the next game. One of the trees can be the new moth.

something else to try:

- If there are lots of players, try playing with more than one bat and moth in the circle.
- Have each bat and moth use a noisemaker (such as a can with some pebbles in it) instead of shouting "bat" or "moth."

65

make a bat-wing kite

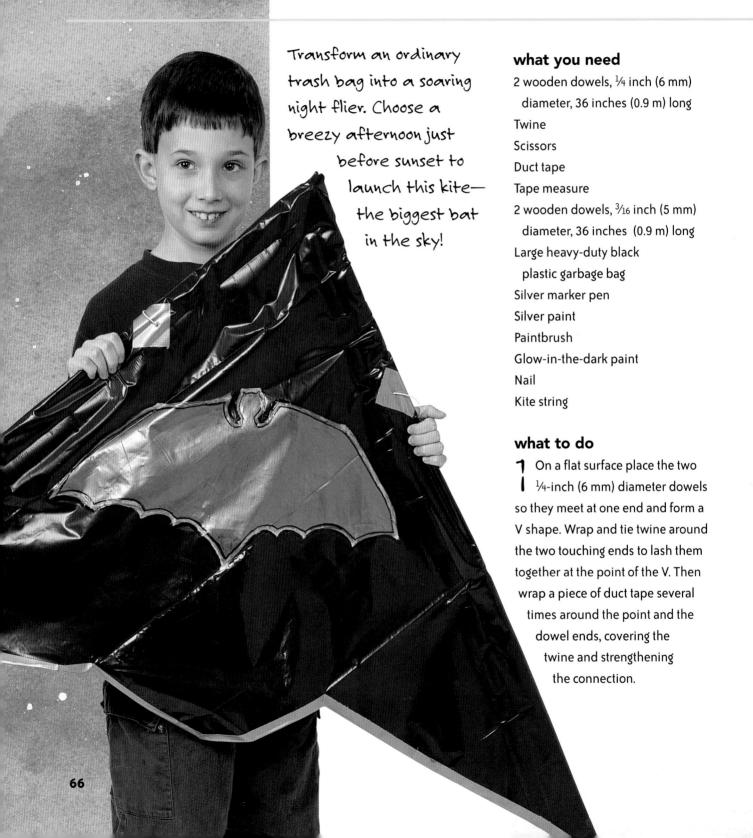

Transform an ordinary trash bag into a soaring night flier. Choose a breezy afternoon just before sunset to launch this kite— the biggest bat in the sky!

what you need

2 wooden dowels, ¼ inch (6 mm) diameter, 36 inches (0.9 m) long
Twine
Scissors
Duct tape
Tape measure
2 wooden dowels, ³⁄₁₆ inch (5 mm) diameter, 36 inches (0.9 m) long
Large heavy-duty black plastic garbage bag
Silver marker pen
Silver paint
Paintbrush
Glow-in-the-dark paint
Nail
Kite string

what to do

1 On a flat surface place the two ¼-inch (6 mm) diameter dowels so they meet at one end and form a V shape. Wrap and tie twine around the two touching ends to lash them together at the point of the V. Then wrap a piece of duct tape several times around the point and the dowel ends, covering the twine and strengthening the connection.

2 Now, measure 7 inches (17.8 cm) straight down from the tip of the V. Lay one of the 3/16-inch (5 mm) diameter dowels across the frame at the 7-inch mark and cut or snap the dowel to fit between the V's sides at that point. Lash it to the sides of the frame with twine. Likewise, place, cut, and lash the second dowel across the frame 18 inches (45.7 cm) straight down from the point of the V (see figure 1).

3 With scissors cut along the seam of one side and across the bottom of the garbage bag to open it up. Then spread the plastic out flat. Place the frame on the plastic with the point of the V in one corner and with 2 to 3 inches of plastic around the frame's outside edges (see figure 2).

4 Double over the extra plastic and fold it over the sides along the kite frame. Use strips of duct tape to hold the folds in place. Be sure to smooth the plastic and keep it taut under the kite frame as you work around it. When you come to the crossbars, fold the plastic over them and secure it

Figure 1

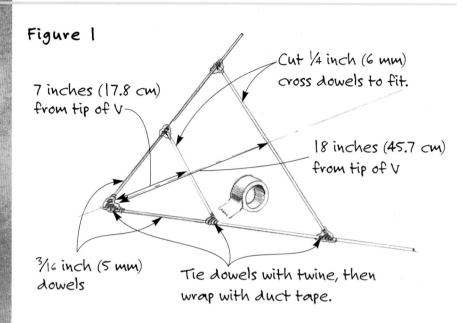

7 inches (17.8 cm) from tip of V

Cut 1/4 inch (6 mm) cross dowels to fit.

18 inches (45.7 cm) from tip of V

3/16 inch (5 mm) dowels

Tie dowels with twine, then wrap with duct tape.

Figure 2

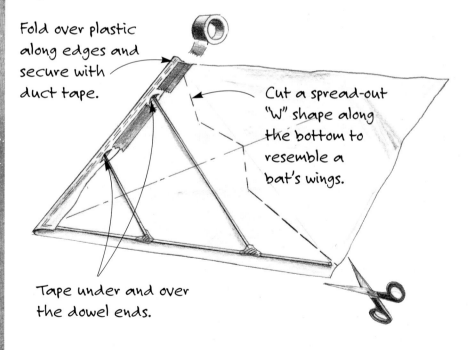

Fold over plastic along edges and secure with duct tape.

Cut a spread-out "W" shape along the bottom to resemble a bat's wings.

Tape under and over the dowel ends.

with tape. Then place an extra piece of tape under and over each crossbar to strengthen the area. (The tape forms a pocket here; see figure 2.)

5 Cut a sloping, open W shape along the bottom of the kite to make it resemble a bat's wings (see figure 2). Then line the cut edge with a thin strip of tape (see the photo, page 66).

6 Use a silver marker pen to draw the shape of a bat on top of the kite. Paint the bat with two coats of silver paint. Then outline the edges of the bat with glow-in-the-dark paint.

7 Now it's time to attach the kite's string. First, you'll need to strengthen the areas where the string meets the kite. Measure 11 inches (28 cm) down from the point of the kite on each of the two sides of the V and place a square piece of tape there on

top of the kite, over the plastic-covered dowel. Then use a nail to poke a hole through each patch, as well as through the plastic and the tape below, as close to the frame as possible. Pass the end of the kite string down through one hole, across the

bottom of the kite, and up through the hole on the opposite side. Then tie the string's free end to the string itself, centered on the underside of the kite, so that it forms a triangular loop (see figure 3).

 Go fly your kite!

Figure 3

Poke a hole and pass string through reinforced plastic.

Extra square of tape 11 inches (28 cm) down from the point of the "V" on both sides to reinforce areas.

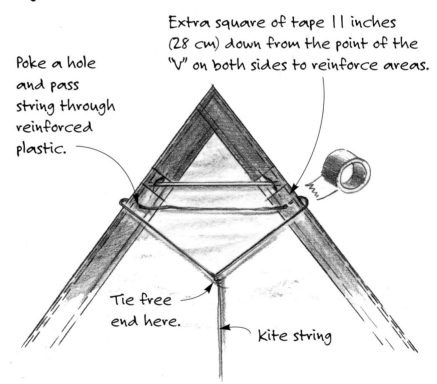

Tie free end here.

Kite string

the fly-by-nights

Not all birds sleep the night away. If you look carefully, you'll get a glimpse of nature's after-dark birds: the night fliers. Owls swoop the skies searching for easy prey. Nighthawks scoop up insects in midair. Whippoorwills and mockingbirds sing out. And high overhead, thousands of moon birds soar. *Moon birds?* Read on to find out more . . .

amazing owls

Eyes looking for a prize, this long-eared owl swoops silently through the darkness in search of prey. It folds its feathery ear tufts down when it flies.

Shhhhh . . . listen! Way over there in your neighbor's yard, by that tree on the far side, underneath that pile of leaves: can you hear the footsteps of a tiny mouse? Of course you can't. But an owl can, even while flying high in the air in the dark.

With a quick swoop and a grab of razor-sharp claws, *squeeeek*—that mouse would become the owl's dinner. Gulp, swallow, no more mouse. Owls eat their mice whole!

Owls are to the night what hawks and eagles are to the day. They eat the same kinds of food—mostly mice, and also bugs, toads, snakes, and other small animals. But they use the night to find it. By hunting and eating during different parts of the 24-hour day, different kinds of creatures can share the same food supply without having to fight over it.

SUPER SEEING

Owls can see 35 to 100 times better in the dark than humans. One reason why is that owls have H-U-G-E eyes compared to the size of their bodies. If your eyes were as big compared to your body, they'd be the size of grapefruits and weigh 5 pounds (2.3 kg) each.

One thing owl eyes *can't* do is move around in their sockets from side to side or up or down, like your eyes can. Owls can look only straight forward (which is why they always seem to be staring). So instead of moving its eyes to look around, an owl moves its whole head. Special neck bones let an owl swivel its head three-fourths of a full circle. If you had a swivel neck like an owl's, you could turn your head all the way around until you were looking straight behind you, and then keep on turning for another quarter-turn. Go ahead and try it now . . . *ouch!*

QUIET AS A MOUSE? *QUIETER.*

How does an owl sneak up on a mouse? *Very quietly.* Noisy wings flapping would scare prey away. But a flying owl makes almost no sound at all. Its extra-big wings help it glide silently. And its soft, fringed wing feathers muffle the sound of air passing over them.

SUPER-ER HEARING

Even with such great eyesight, owls mostly use their amazing hearing power to find prey in the dark. Owls have better hearing than any other kind of bird— and maybe any other kind of animal, period. Some types of owls can hear a mouse squeak half a mile (805 m) away.

An owl's entire face is specially shaped for hearing. The feathers on each side of its face form a sound-catching funnel, like the dish-shaped antennas used for receiving satellite TV signals. But instead of hearing soap operas and game shows, owl ears pick up telltale rustles, squeaks, and other sounds made by small animals.

Underneath its face feathers are the owl's ear openings. They're much bigger than yours, and the opening on one side is higher than the opening on the other side. That way the owl can tell whether a sound is coming from the right or left or from higher or lower, and can zoom to that exact spot. When hunting, an owl moves its head back and forth to help zero in on sounds. An owl can even grab a meal hidden beneath deep snow.

These barn owls have facial feathers that form discs, like dish-shaped antennas, that funnel sound into their ear openings.

WHAT A HOOT!

Owls are the original stealth fliers: swift, whisper-quiet, and camouflaged. They're almost impossible to see in the dark. But they make sounds—hoots and yelps and other calls—to attract mates or claim territory. So you're way more likely to *hear* an owl calling at night than to see one perched or flying. You can still tell what sort of owl it is, though, because every kind makes its own special sounds.

Use the chart here to figure out just *whoooo* that owl is you're hearing.

owl	sound
Great horned owl	Hoo hoo-hoo hoo hooooo
Barn owl	Sssssssssshhhh (like a loud hissing snake)
Barred owl	Hoo hoo hoo-hoo, hoo hoo hoo-hoo-aww
Eastern screech owl	Eeeeeeeeeeeeeee (shaky whistle, like a horse's whinny but higher pitched)
Western screech owl	Oooo oooo oooh-oooh oooo-oooh-oooh-oooh (with a rhythm like a bouncing ping pong ball)
Long-eared owl	Woooo (repeats about every three seconds)

Barred owls have dark eyes and no feathery "horns." Owls can't move their eyes, so they always look like they're gazing straight into yours.

FINDING OWLS

- Your best chance of seeing an owl at night is when there's a bright moon and little wind. Listen for their calls and try to locate the sound.
- Look especially in places where there's a mixture of both trees and open areas. That's where most common owls hunt.
- During the day, if you hear a bunch of crows or other birds making a lot of noise and circling around one area, follow the sound. Day birds don't like owls near their nests and will raise a ruckus, flying around it and screeching and scolding. If you're lucky, you'll get a look at the owl before they chase it away.

are owls really wise?

With their big, all-knowing eyes, owls certainly look wise. And there's no doubt they're super-sharp when it comes to seeing and hearing. Actually, that's why owls are not particularly wise or smart. An owl's huge eyeballs and ear openings take up so much space in its skull there's only a little room left for a brain.

All energy and fluff, month-old baby screech owls leave the nest before they can fly, but stay together near their parents, who feed them. They hop from branch to branch, practicing for flight.

what's in an owl's dinner?

An owl doesn't have teeth, so instead of chewing, it swallows its prey whole. Inside the owl's stomach the soft fleshy parts get digested, but the other, harder stuff—like bones and fur and claws—form into a pellet. Then the owl spits the pellet out onto the ground below its perch. Owls spit out about two pellets a day. Scientists pick apart owl pellets to figure out what owls eat. You can do the same. Owl pellets aren't squishy or gross. They're dry and safe to handle (just wash your hands afterward—or if you'd rather, wear gloves while handling them).

How do you get pellets? Owls usually roost in the same places, so if you find an owl's favorite tree you can find the pellets it spit out. Look for a large tree with "whitewash" on the trunk (where the owl pooped while roosting). Look carefully on the ground below for pellets. You can also buy pellets by mail order or at nature centers.

what you need
Owl pellet
Small bowl of warm water
   (optional; see Note)
Dishwashing detergent
      (optional; see Note)
      Paper towels
      Tweezers
      Toothpicks or pencils

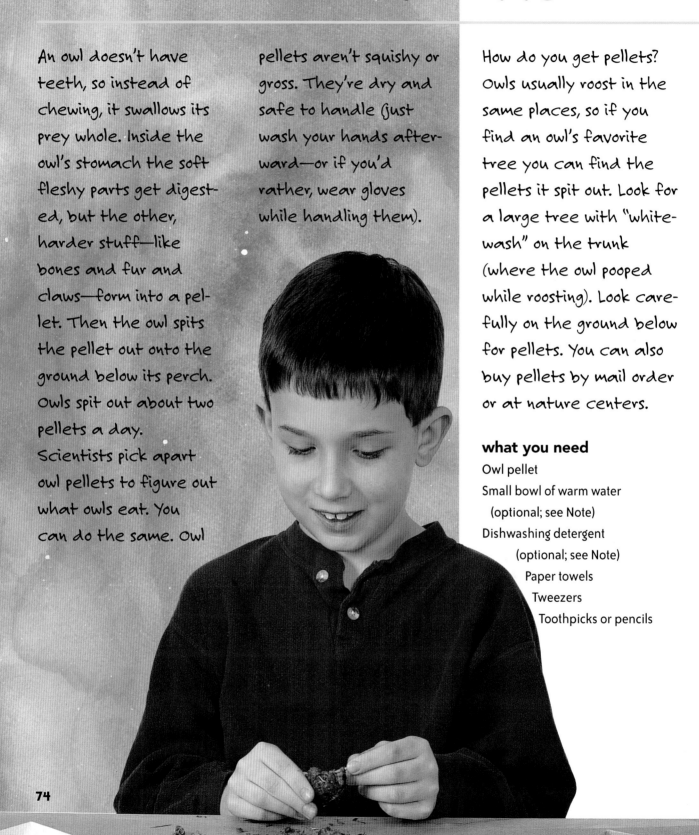

what to do

Note: If the pellet is especially hard and tough, you'll need to soften it first. Put a drop of dishwashing detergent in a small bowl of warm water, then add the pellet. Let the pellet soak for about an hour.

1 Put the pellet on some paper towels. Using the tweezers and toothpicks or pencils (and your fingers too) carefully pick and pull apart the pellet.

2 Separate the fur, bones, and other pieces, putting each type in its own pile or group.

3 Study the different pieces to figure out what the owl ate. Did you find a tiny skull with teeth? It probably came from a mouse or other small animal. Do any of the bones fit together? Did you find feathers or a beak from a bird?

4 What can you figure out from the pieces? Did the owl eat more than one kind of food? How many kinds? What was the biggest meal? What was the smallest?

5 Pick apart more pellets and compare them to the others. Do larger pellets contain more meals, or just bigger creatures?

something else to try:

- Collect pellet bones. You can specialize in just one kind, such as skulls or teeth. Or you can keep all the bones from a single pellet and try to rebuild the animals' skeletons.
- Use a field guide to mammal bones to help you identify the animals you find in pellets.

mouse bones you might find

The drawings here show some typical mouse bones you might find in an owl pellet.

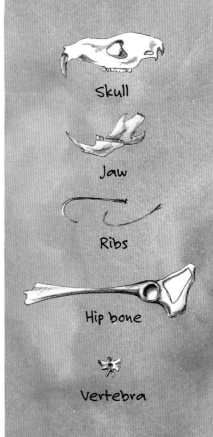

Skull

Jaw

Ribs

Hip bone

Vertebra

build a screech owl house

what you need

A grownup to help you (see Note), plus:

MATERIALS & SUPPLIES

1 X 10 pine shelving board, 8 feet (2.4 m) long (see Note 2)

1 X 2 pine furring strip, 8 feet long (2.4 m) (see Note 2)

6 x 6-inch (15.2 x 15.2 cm) square of aluminum window screen or plastic needlepoint netting

Medium-grit sandpaper

Masking or duct tape (optional)

Tube of waterproof outdoor wood glue

20 1⅝-inch (4.1 cm) galvanized outdoor decking screws

2 6D galvanized outdoor common nails

1 pair of 2-inch (5 cm) brass or zinc-coated hinges

Exterior latex house paint, gray

Hardwood or pine wood shavings (sold at pet stores)

2 rubber bungee cords

TOOLS

Tape measure

Ruler or carpenter's square

Pencil

Handsaw or power saw

Power drill with ½-inch (1.3 cm) and ⅛-inch (3 mm) drill bits

Heavy-duty staple gun with ⅜- or ½-inch (9.5 mm or 1.3 cm) staples

3-inch (7.6 cm) hole saw attachment for drill or a small keyhole handsaw

Screwdriver or power drill with screwdriver bit (recommended)

Hammer

Paintbrush

Screech owls are small night fliers with big appetites for mice and other rodents. Their soft, trembling whistles fill the night with eerie mystery. Build this simple owl house to invite a screech owl family to your neighborhood.

Doesn't give a hoot: Screech owls don't hoot like other owls. Listen for their high, shaky whistles after sunset.

Cutting Diagram

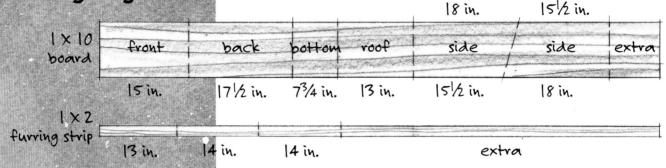

1 X 10 board
front | back | bottom | roof | side | side | extra

18 in.   15½ in.

15 in.   17½ in.   7¾ in.   13 in.   15½ in.   18 in.

1 X 2 furring strip

13 in.   14 in.   14 in.   extra

Note: To convert to metrics, multiply the measurement in inches by 2.54 to determine centimeters or by 25.40 for millimeters.

what to do

Note: You'll need a grownup to help you choose and measure the materials for your owl house and also to help with the sawing, drilling, and other steps that require power tools. Your helper will come in handy for holding parts while you screw them together, too, and for mounting the owl house high up in a tree.

Note 2: The actual dimensions of a 1 X 10 board are ¾ x 9¼ inches (1.9 x 23.5 cm). The actual dimensions of a 1 X 2 furring strip are ¾ x 1½ inches (1.9 x 3.8 cm).

1 Using the tape measure, ruler or square, and a pencil, measure and mark the cut lines for the owl house parts on the pine shelving board as shown above. Measure and mark the pine furring strip, too, as shown.

2 Use the saw to cut the pieces you've marked. Lightly write each part's name (bottom, back, etc.) on the pieces as you cut them to help you keep track of them.

3 Drill a ½-inch (1.3 cm) hole 1 inch (2.5 cm) in from each end of the two 14-inch (35.6 cm) pieces of furring strip. These pieces, together with the bungee cords, will hold your owl house to the tree.

4 Drill a square of four equally spaced ½-inch (1.3 cm) holes near the center of the bottom board, as shown in the drawing on page 76. These are for drainage. Then staple the square of screen or netting over the holes on one side of the board.

5 Now it's time to drill the entrance hole for the house. Measure and mark 3½ inches (8.9 cm) down from the top center of the front board. Then drill the entrance hole at that spot using a power drill with a 3-inch (7.6 cm) hole saw attachment. Or, drill a ½-inch (1.3 cm) hole at the mark and then use a keyhole handsaw to cut out a 3-inch circle by hand. The hole doesn't have to be a perfect circle, but it does need to be about 3 inches high and wide and not too lopsided in any direction.

6 Using sandpaper, sand all the pieces lightly, making sure to smooth any rough edges.

Screech Owl House (Exploded View)

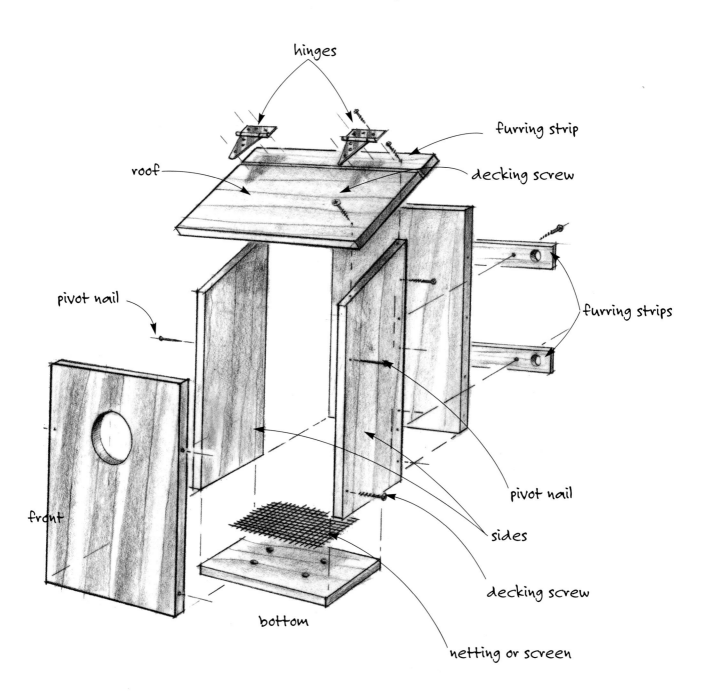

hinges

furring strip

decking screw

roof

furring strips

pivot nail

pivot nail

front

sides

decking screw

bottom

netting or screen

7 Lay all the parts out in front of you and study the drawing (left) until you're sure you understand how everything goes together. Sometimes it helps to actually assemble all the pieces using masking or duct tape to hold them in place. This lets you see how the panels fit together before you actually glue and screw them. When you've studied how everything fits, remove the tape.

8 Spread some glue along one long edge of the bottom panel and press the lower inside end of the back panel against it. Then screw the pieces together using three screws.

9 Next, attach the two sides to the assembled back and bottom panels, again using glue and screws. Be sure the highest corner of each side is level with the top of the back. The sides should extend beyond the front edge of the bottom panel.

10 Now slip the front panel with the entrance hole in place between the two sides and against the bottom panel. The front panel's bottom edge should be even with the bottom edges

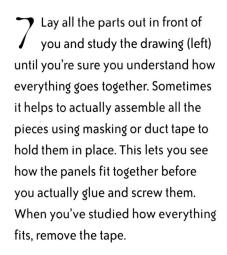

of the two sides. DO NOT GLUE the front panel in place. This will be a swing-out door to make cleaning your owl house easy.

11 Drill a ⅛-inch (3 mm) hole through each of the two sides into the side edges of the front panel. The holes should be exactly the same distance from the top on both sides, about 4½ inches (11.4 cm).

12 Gently hammer into each hole one of the 6D nails until the head is flush with the surface of the side. These nails act as pivots for swinging out the front. Push the front

Pour a layer of wood shavings into your owl house before you hang it. The mother screech owl will use the wood shavings as a nest to lay her eggs on and raise her babies.

panel in at the top and pull it out at the bottom to make sure it swings freely.

13 Now attach the two 14-inch (35.6 cm) furring strip pieces across the back of the box. Position one strip across the upper back and the other toward the bottom. Glue and screw them in place, making sure the screws go into the side edges and not the back panel.

14 Position the 13-inch (33 cm) furring strip even with the back upper edge of the top of the box. Be sure it overhangs evenly left and right. Use glue and two screws to attach it securely. Drive the screws into the side's top edges.

15 Put the roof panel in place, lining it up evenly with the 13-inch (33 cm) furring strip. DO NOT GLUE the roof to the sides. Instead, attach the roof to the 13-inch furring strip with hinges spaced evenly, about ½ inch (1.3 cm) in from each side.

16 Drive a decking screw down through the roof and into the top edge of the right side panel (see the drawing). Then back the screw out until you can open the roof again. Likewise, drive another screw

through the right side panel and into the side edge of the front panel. Keep this screw tightened for now. Use these two screws to open and close the roof and front door when you need to clean the house.

17 Paint your owl house with gray latex exterior house paint or stain.

18 Open the roof and pour in a layer of wood shavings 2 to 3 inches (5 to 7.6 cm) deep. Screech owls need a layer of wood shavings to use as a soft nest. Then close the roof and tighten down the screw that holds it in place.

19 Hang your owl house 15 feet (4.5 m) or higher in a large tree in or along the edge of a wooded area. Use the bungee cords to reach around the tree, hooking them into the holes in the back furring strips. If the cords are too long, just tie knots in them to make them shorter.

20 Watch for signs of life around your owl house. Sometimes other creatures, such as

gray squirrels or flying squirrels, will use the house instead. Once a year, in late fall or winter, climb up and open the door and roof of your owl house. Clean out the old wood shavings and replace them with new. Don't open the box if you know owls are still living there, though. Also, if you find nesting materials such as leaves, moss, or sticks, this means another creature has been nesting there. Never disturb an active nest.

other birds in the night: goatsuckers, mockers—and moon birds?

Owls aren't the only birds that come out when the Sun goes down. Keep your exploring eyes (and ears) open for these other secretive feathered friends.

GOATSUCKERS

Uck! What kind of bird could a *goat-sucker* be? Actually, this group of perfectly okay birds got its name from an old, silly superstition that they feed on the milk of goats at night (*wrong*). Goatsuckers all have a leafy camouflage pattern that hides them during the day as they rest on the ground or along a branch. They also have large mouths surrounded by long, stiff whiskers. The whiskers form a funnel that helps the birds scoop insects into their mouths while they're flying.

Goatsuckers include the common nighthawk, the whippoorwill, the poorwill, and the chuck-will's-widow. The last three are all named for the sounds they make—and are also called nightjars, because they make such night-jarring noise. For example, the whippoorwill's call is a whistling *whip-poor-will, whip-poor-will, whip-poor-will* repeated over and over (and *over* and *over*)—as many as 16,000 times in one night! Nightjars perch patiently on the ground or a low branch until an insect flies by, then—whoosh—they take off and gobble up the food.

Common nighthawks hunt by soaring the evening skies continuously, zooming high and low, back and forth, catching insects in their wide-open mouths. Look for their pointed, swept-back wings with white bars on the underside. They often fly around floodlights, gulping bugs, at nighttime baseball or soccer games.

Be-leaf it or not, there's a bird in this photo! The whippoorwill here, like other members of the goatsucker family, is so well camouflaged it's almost invisible.

Singing day and night, northern mockingbirds imitate parts of other birdsongs. Each bird sings its own combination of up to 300 different tunes and always repeats it the same way.

MOCKINGBIRDS

The mockingbird's a day bird that doesn't know when to quit. Perched high on a roof or in a treetop, it sings during the day—and keeps right on singing at night, when other songbirds are asleep. It's called a *mockingbird* because it imitates other birdsongs. The mockingbird repeats parts of different songs, singing each part four or more times, then changing to another song, and another, and so on, sometimes for hours. Mockingbirds also sometimes imitate other sounds—a dog barking, a cat meowing, sirens, even squeaky doors!

Many birds migrate at night. By counting the number of birds that pass across the full moon, you can figure out how many birds are in the night sky.

TRAVELERS PASSING THROUGH

In fall, when the weather turns colder, many birds *migrate* south to spend the winter in warmer places where there's more food to eat. In spring, they come back by flying north. Millions of birds take to the skies and fly hundreds of miles during these migrations.

So why don't you see these huge rivers of birds flying south in fall and returning north in spring? Because many birds—not just owls, but many day birds, too—migrate after dark, while you're sleeping. Sparrows, wrens, thrushes, geese, warblers, and hundreds more use the night to fly to their summer and winter homes. The night sky makes traveling easier. The weather's cooler and calmer, there are fewer enemies such as hawks, and night flying leaves the daytime free for eating and resting.

Sometimes you can see night-migrating birds just before dark and in the early morning. Also, if you listen carefully on calm spring and autumn nights, you might hear the chirps and twitters of migrating birds—thousands of them—passing overhead in the night sky. You can also try Count "Moon Birds" on the next page.

count "moon birds"

Three hundred years ago, people believed that birds flew to the moon in fall and spent the winter there. Of course, now we know better. But as a night explorer you actually can see birds "on" the moon during their migrations. Until recently, watching and counting birds passing in front of the Moon was an important way for scientists to study how many birds were migrating. Today scientists mostly use radar for their research. But counting "moon birds" is still interesting and fun.

what you need

Full moon in spring or autumn

Binoculars or telescope

Watch

Notepad

Pencil

what to do

1 Find a place where you have a good view of the entire Moon through your binoculars or telescope.

2 Watch carefully for the dark outlines, or silhouettes, of birds passing across the disc of the Moon in the night sky.

3 Count the number of "moon birds" you see within 15 minutes. Write the number down in your notebook. Do this three more times, so you've watched for a total of one hour and have written down four "moon bird" counts.

4 Add the numbers to get the number of "moon birds" per hour.

5 Multiply that number by 347 (the full moon takes up about $\frac{1}{347}$th of the visible night sky).

6 The number you get is roughly the number of migrating birds that flew across the night sky in the last hour.

example:

Number of moon birds sighted

First 15 minutes: 4

Second 15 minutes: 9

Third 15 minutes: 2

Fourth 15 minutes: 5

4 + 9 + 2 + 5 = 20 times 347 = 6,940 birds per hour

something else to try:

Use a portable tape recorder to record the sounds of migrating birds passing overhead. Try to identify which kinds of birds they are by comparing the sounds on your recording to bird-call tapes or CDs from the library.

insects in the night

Some fly quietly to a porch light or window screen, silent visitors from an unseen world. Some arrive noisily, buzzing and bumbling and bouncing like buggy, clumsy clowns. Some light up the night with their own little lanterns. Moths, fireflies, and other insects fill the night with all sorts of sights and sounds. The ones you see and hear are only a few of the zillions of nighttime fliers, creepers, and crawlers that live in your neighborhood. How many kinds are out there? What are they doing and why are they doing it? How can you get a closer look? Let's find out!

moths: butterflies of the night

What's a moth? You probably think of a small, brownish flying bug flopping around a porch light—or zooming straight into a campfire (poof!). Many moths *are* small and brown. But there are lots of others, too, in all sorts of colors, patterns, shapes, and sizes.

In fact, there are more kinds of moths in our world than all the species of birds, reptiles, mammals, and fish combined. Some moths are as small as . . . well, as the word "as" on this page. Some have wings wider than your hand.

Here's another amazing fact: There are over 14 times more moths flying around than butterflies! In North America there are at least 11,000 kinds of moths, and only about 750 kinds of butterflies.

So why do we notice butterflies more often? Because we're asleep when most moths are out. Besides, butterflies are daytime showoffs. They're bright and colorful and easy to see. Moths are daytime hiders. They rest quietly on tree trunks and in leaves and bushes. Many are camouflaged. Their soft colors and wing patterns help them blend into their surroundings by imitating bird droppings, leaves, lichens, and tree bark. They're hard for predators—and people—to see.

LIFE'S CHANGES

If you think *you've* changed a lot since you were born . . . well, you're right. But moths change even more. They start out as totally different creatures.

Moths, like many other insects, begin life as eggs and go through a series of changes called *complete metamorphosis*. First, each moth egg hatches into a small larva, or caterpillar. All moths spend the first few days or weeks of their lives as caterpillars, eating and building energy.

Moth caterpillars eat a *lot*. They grow so fast they have to molt, or shed their skin, several times to make room for their bigger bodies.

In its first nine weeks a polyphemus (pahl-uh-FEE-muss) moth caterpillar eats 86,000 times its own birth weight in leaves. Eventually it grows to 3 inches (7.6 cm) long and as big around as your finger.

Next, the caterpillar becomes a pupa. It rests, not eating or

Beast to beauty: A moth caterpillar looks nothing like the winged moth it will become. The weird caterpillar above (top) becomes a beautiful polyphemus silk moth (upper left). And this spiny caterpillar (bottom) changes into the lovely Io moth on page 86.

Yipes! Big eyes! I'm outta here! The Io moth's animal-like eyespots scare away predators (sometimes).

moth "nose"

Male moths have large, feathery antennae to help them find mates. Each little branch on the antennae is covered with tiny hairs that detect the special scent given off by females of the same species.

moving, and slowly changes into an adult moth. Sphinx moth larvae burrow underground and harden into pupae. Many other moths pupate inside a cocoon made of leaves, or of silk they spin around themselves.

Some moths pupate for just a few days. Others, like the polyphemus, sleep through an entire winter. Meanwhile, the moth's body changes. It grows wings, antennae, and internal organs.

When it's ready, the insect pushes out of its shelter—ta da, an adult moth! It slowly flaps its droopy wings to pump blood into them. Gradually the wings stretch to full size and stiffen. The moth flutters away to find a mate.

An adult moth doesn't live long—usually just a few days. Its whole purpose is to mate. Some kinds don't even eat or drink. Others sip water, nectar, or tree sap.

After mating, a female moth lays her eggs on the kinds of plants or other food sources preferred by baby caterpillars of her species. Giant leopard moths lay their eggs on dandelion or honeysuckle leaves. Luna moth caterpillars like hickory leaves. Wax moths lay their eggs in beehives.

SUPER SENSES

How do moth mates find one another in the dark? The female stays in one place and gives off a special scent, called a *pheromone*, that attracts males of her species. The male finds her by following his "nose." Sense organs on his feathery antennae pick up traces of her pheromone in the air. Using his super sniffer, a male polyphemus moth can find a female up to five miles (8.3 km) away.

Moths have sensitive eyes, too, that help them locate mates or food sources. If you shine a flashlight on a moth in the dark, its eyes sparkle with reflected eye shine.

SCARY WINGS

Most moths have special wing patterns to help them hide. But some moths also use their wings to scare enemies. If a bird comes too close to an underwing moth, it suddenly lifts its dark, drab wings and—yikes!— flashes bright red- or orange-striped bottom wings. The trick startles the bird long enough for the moth to escape. Other moths have a different sort of surprise ready for predators. When they pull their forewings forward they reveal two large spots that resemble scary animal eyes. *Boo!*

FRIEND OR FIEND?

Some kinds of moth larvae are pests. Tomato hornworms and corn earworms gobble up crops in gardens and on farms. House moth larvae nibble holes in wool (hey, that's my sweater you're eating!). Most moths and moth caterpillars, though, are harmless and an important food source for birds, bats, fish, snakes, bears, mice, and even other insects.

MOTH FAMILIES

Some moths are more alike than others, so scientists have put similar kinds into groups. Here are three major moth families.

giant silk moths

Giant silk moths are some of the biggest and most beautiful moths. The pale green luna, the polyphemus, the cecropia, and the Io moth are some examples. There are about 70 kinds of silk moths in North America, but only six in Europe.

sphinx moths

Sphinx moths are also called hawk moths and are the fastest flying of all butterflies and moths. The white-lined sphinx can zoom up to 30 miles (48 km) an hour! Many sphinx moths fly during the day, sipping nectar from flowers and hovering like hummingbirds. There are about 120 kinds of sphinx moths.

tiger moths

If you've ever seen a woolly bear caterpillar, you were actually looking at a tiger-moth-to-be. After spending the winter frozen solid, a woolly bear caterpillar (right, top) becomes an Isabella tiger moth (right, bottom). There are at least 200 different kinds of tiger moths.

Whrrrr, sip, zip! The white-lined sphinx moth flies and sounds like a hummingbird.

The woolly bear caterpillar becomes a fuzzy-headed Isabella tiger moth.

The cecropia is the largest silk moth in North America. Its wings can be almost 6 inches (15.2 cm) wide.

WHERE TO LOOK FOR MOTHS

Look for day-flying sphinx moths around flowers in meadows and yards. Bright lights near campgrounds and in parks are good places to search for underwing moths and giant silk moths. Or, you can get moths to come to you. Try attracting them with moth goop (see Go "Sugaring" for Moths on the next page) or make the light-and-sheet insect collector on page 97.

key shaking for moths

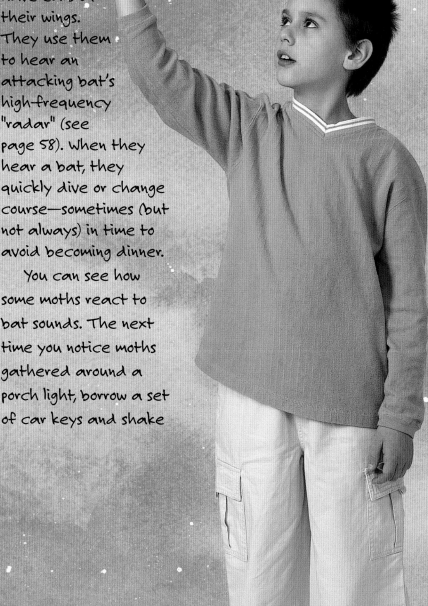

Besides having powerful senses of sight and smell, many moths also have extra-sensitive ears. Some moths have ears on their bodies, and others have ears on their wings. They use them to hear an attacking bat's high-frequency "radar" (see page 58). When they hear a bat, they quickly dive or change course—sometimes (but not always) in time to avoid becoming dinner.

You can see how some moths react to bat sounds. The next time you notice moths gathered around a porch light, borrow a set of car keys and shake them lightly. The jingling keys create ultrasonic vibrations similar to a bat's. If there are any bat-sensitive moths around, they'll scatter fast!

go "sugaring" for moths

To get moths to come to you, mix up a mess of moth goop. It's sticky, it's stinky—and moths love it!

what you need

1 almost-rotten banana

Bowl

Spoon

2 ounces (60 mL) of apple cider vinegar

½ pound (227 g) of brown sugar

Plastic wrap

Small bucket

Wide paintbrush

Flashlight

Red plastic wrap or tissue paper

what to do

1 Peel the banana and put it in the bowl. Mash it with the spoon until it's gloppy, like paste.

2 Add the vinegar and brown sugar and mix them together completely with the banana. Warning: Hold your nose! This stuff stinks! The mixture should be about as thick as house paint. If it's too runny, mash and add another banana.

3 Cover the bowl with plastic wrap and put it in a warm place indoors for several hours or overnight.

4 Find a place where there are several trees at the edge of an open space. A meadow next to woods is good. So is your yard if there are lots of trees and bushes.

5 A warm, still, cloudy night is best for moth "sugar-ing." Just before sunset, pour the moth goop into the bucket. Then use the brush to paint a good, thick coating of goop about half the size of this page onto the bark of several trees.

6 A few hours after dark, go outside and check your trees for goop-guzzling moths. If you're lucky you'll see several on each tree. Use a flashlight covered with red plastic wrap or tissue paper so you won't bother the moths as they feed.

7 Moths like moth goop because it resembles the sugary tree sap they find in nature. You'll probably see ants, beetles, and other insects licking up the goop also. Be sure to take time to watch them, too. Use a field guide to figure out the kinds of moths and other bugs you're seeing.

plant a moonlight moth garden

Bees and butterflies visit daytime flowers. At night, day flowers close, and night flowers open to give nectar-feeding moths a sip. This moveable moth garden lets you put it where you can see the flowers and watch the action.

what you need

Small stones or gravel
Large planter pot
Potting soil
Night-blooming flower seeds
   (available at garden stores)
Long stick
Watering can
Water

what to do

1 Put a layer of stones or gravel in the bottom of the planter pot. The stones help keep the soil from getting too wet.

2 Fill the planter halfway with potting soil. Pat the soil down lightly to get rid of extra air spaces. Then fill the pot the rest of the way with soil and pat the dirt again.

3 Choose seeds for one or more kinds of night-blooming flowers (see the examples on the next page) and plant them in the soil according to the instructions on the seed packet.

4 Use the watering can to moisten the soil thoroughly with water. Be careful not to pour too much water at once or the soil covering the seeds will wash away. Instead, sprinkle on just a little water at a time, wait a minute for the water to soak in, then sprinkle on some more.

5 If any of the seeds you planted will grow into vines, push a long stick into the soil near them so the plants will have something to climb.

6 Put the planter in a spot where the flowers will get the sun or shade they need (the seed packets will tell you which) and where you'll be able to watch the flowers and moths at night. Your planter will be heavy, so ask a grownup to help you move it.

7 Check your garden every day. Keep the soil moist (but not soaking wet) until the seeds sprout.

90

8 When the seeds come up, pull out any "extra" plants that are too close together so the flowers will have enough room to grow.

9 Take care of your midnight moth garden just as you would any garden. Keep it watered and weeded.

10 When the plants are fully grown, watch them open just before or after the sun goes down. Can you smell them? Most night-blooming flowers are especially fragrant to attract moths. Speaking of which—wow! Did you see those hawkmoths zipping around your flowers?

night-blooming garden flowers

Night-blooming flowers such as these have sweet-scented white or light-colored blossoms to attract moths. Night-exploring humans like them, too.

moonflower   evening primrose

four o'clocks   night phlox   nicotiana

fireflies: the twinkle in nature's eye

Blink . . . flash . . . blink blink . . .
if you've seen fireflies flashing in the night, you know how magical they seem—like tiny, floating lights drifting in air. Well, the truth is, fireflies *are* magical in many ways. Scientists are still trying to figure them out.

There are almost 2,000 different kinds of fireflies. Actually, they're not flies at all. They're flying beetles, members of a family called Lampryidae, which means "shining fire." Not all parts of the world are lucky enough to have them. For instance, there are no fireflies at all in Europe or in very dry places such as the American Southwest. Fireflies live in most other regions of the United States, though. There are about 100 kinds in North America.

NIGHT COURTING

Where there are fireflies, there are usually at least five or six different kinds, or species, sharing the same territory. Each kind has its own special pattern of flashing so that males and females of the same species can find each other in the dark.

The male pyralis firefly, for instance, always swoops upward as he flashes, making a little J of light. He swoops and flashes about every six seconds. Male scintillating fireflies fly straight and level, blinking single flashes over and over. Pennsylvania firefly males perch among the treetops and make four or five quick flashes in a row.

In fact, all the fireflies you see flying and flashing in the air at night are males. The females stay on the ground or in a low bush.

When a female spies a male firefly winking her kind of wink, she waits just the right amount of time for her species and then answers back with the right kind of flash. For instance, a female pyralis firefly

Fireflies aren't flies at all. They're beetles. Beneath this firefly's wings is its tiny flashy "light bulb."

flashes back about two seconds after the male. Then the male answers her with his J. She waits again and answers him, and so on.

As the fireflies "talk," the male comes closer and closer. But the two don't always end up mating. Males that flash faster or brighter than the average firefly may get a super-bright reaction from the female. But less impressive males may get a cold shoulder—a ho-hum dim blink—or no more talk at all. (Get lost, buddy!)

After mating, the female firefly lays her eggs on damp moss or grass. When the eggs hatch, the little worm-like larvae glow constantly. That's why they're called glowworms.

LIGHT FACTORY

The light fireflies make is called *bioluminesence*—light created by a chemical reaction inside a living thing. Some kinds of mushrooms, algae, and other organisms are bioluminescent, too. But the firefly is the world's most famous living light maker.

How does the light happen? A firefly's "lantern" is made of two layers inside its abdomen. One layer is a reflector, to make the light brighter. The other layer produces two special chemicals, luciferin and luciferase. When the chemicals combine with oxygen and the insect's own tissues, they give off energy in the form of—you guessed it—light. Whoa, look at the glow!

FIREFLY WATCHING

Fireflies are active in early summer, especially on warm, moist, moonless nights. Watch carefully for the differences between kinds of fireflies. Some kinds come out at dusk. Others don't come out until it's completely dark. Some flash yellow, some green, and some orange. Some float slowly just above the ground. Others cruise at eye level or flit among the treetops. Some kinds of fireflies flash for only about 20 minutes a night. Others flash for hours.

If you're careful not to hurt them, it's okay to catch fireflies in a jar (poke a few holes in the lid) to get a closer look. Just be sure to let them go the same night, after you've finished watching them.

Don't forget to try "talking" to fireflies, too. See the instructions on the next page.

firefly vs light bulb? no contest!

People think the light bulb is a great invention, and it is. But it can't hold a candle to a firefly's lamp. A light bulb loses most of its energy as heat. The firefly's bulb loses almost none. On an efficiency scale of one to 10, the light bulb is a one. The firefly? A 10!

efficiency score
light bulb=1

firefly=10

talking to fireflies

By watching fireflies carefully and imitating their flashes, you can "talk" them into coming closer to you. (Who knows? Maybe they'll teach you how to glow!)

what you need
A small flashlight or a penlight
A grassy lawn or meadow
   with flashing fireflies

what to do

1 Stand quietly and watch the fireflies. The ones flashing while they're flying and moving around are all males. You want to find a female. Look for a flashing firefly that stays in the same place on the ground, or in a low bush. *That's* a female.

2 When you spot her, wait till she flashes again. Does she flash just once or several times? Is the flash long or slow?

3 After you've figured out how she flashes, count the number of seconds between her flashes. (Just count slowly, or say "one elephant, two elephant, three elephant," and so on.)

4 Now you're ready to try imitating a female firefly. Sit in the grass and hold your flashlight so it's pointing into the grass and will make only a small, bug-size light (if the light is too bright, hold a green leaf over it to dim it). Now, turn on the flashlight, imitate the flash you saw, turn it off, and count the same number of seconds you counted between the real female's flashes. Then repeat the flash, count again, flash again, count again, flash—and so on.

5 If you're lucky enough to have figured out the right code, male fireflies will be fooled and start "talking" to you by flashing back and flying closer. Just keep on flashing. Eventually, one will land near your light. Congratulations. You've just had your first firefly conversation!

something else to try:
If you can't find a flashing female, try imitating a male instead. Watch and count his flashes just as you did above, but when you use your flashlight, stand instead of sitting, and move the flashlight to mimic the firefly's movement as it flies. Watch for answering females near the ground.

experiment with "artificial fireflies"

Have you ever used a light stick? When you bend the plastic tube gently, chemicals inside the stick combine and give off energy as beautiful, glowing light with no heat - the same kind of "cool light" that fireflies make. The chemicals inside fireflies and light sticks are different, but they work in similar ways. So you can use light sticks to help answer questions about fireflies. For instance: do you think temperature might affect a firefly's brightness or flash rate? Hmmmm . . .

what you need

Ice cubes

2 pitchers

Cold water

Hot water

2 light sticks

A dark room inside or
  dark night outside

what to do

1 Put some ice cubes in one pitcher and fill it with cold water. Fill the other pitcher with hot water from a faucet. (Don't use boiling water.)

2 Bend each light stick gently (follow the instructions on their wrappers) and give them a shake to make them glow.

3 Hold one light stick in the ice water and one in the hot water and wait a few minutes.

4 The light stick in warm water becomes brighter and the one in ice water gets dimmer. The chemical reaction in the "hot" stick releases more light energy faster than in the "cold" one.

5 Think about this. Do you suppose the same thing might happen with fireflies? Do you think they flash brighter or faster on hot nights? Hint: Scientists say yes. In one study, pyralis fireflies flashed twice as fast at 82° F (27.8° C) as at 65° F (18.3° C). But why take their word for it? Now that you've observed "artificial" fireflies, try the real thing. Count the time between firefly flashes on a mild summer night, when the temperature's between 60 and 70° F (15.6 and 21.1° C), and on a hot night when it's warmer than 75° F (23.9° C). Do your observations agree with the scientists'?

something else to try:

Leave the light sticks in the hot and cold water. Which one loses its glow completely first? Why?

make a light-and-sheet insect collector

If you think your porch light attracts a lot of insects, just wait till you put out this welcome mat for moths and other night insects. Some bugs just can't resist the lure of bright lights.

what you need

Dark, moonless night
An old white bed sheet
Notebook
Pencil

AND EITHER:
(For outside collector)
Rope long enough to tie
  between two trees
Clothespins
Rocks or bricks
A strong, bright flashlight

OR:
(For inside collector)
Tacks or tape for hanging
  sheet over window
Bright indoor lamp near a window

the outside of the window. Then go inside and turn on the lamp.

3 Now wait for your nighttime visitors to show up. (Make sure all other lights around you are turned off.) Insects drawn by the bright light will land on the sheet. Most will stay still as long as the light is on, so you can take your time watching them.

4 Write down your observations. How many kinds of moths and other insects land on the sheet? Using a field guide, can you identify them? Do some kinds move around more than others? In your notebook, sketch the insects you see.

5 When you're finished watching, turn off the lights and give the sheet a gentle shake to encourage the insects to fly to a safe place.

something else to try:

Instead of a regular light, use a black light, which produces ultraviolet light, a kind that human eyes can see only partially but that attracts large numbers of nighttime insects.

what to do

1 There are two ways to make the collector: outside and inside. To make the outside version, tie the rope tightly between two trees and drape the sheet over it so that one end extends a couple of feet (60 cm) out onto the ground. Clip the sheet to the rope with clothespins and weight the end of the sheet near the ground with rocks or bricks to keep the cloth tight. Put the flashlight on the sheet-covered ground and prop it up with a rock or brick so it's pointing at the hanging sheet. Turn the light on. Move the flashlight back or forward if necessary until it casts a dinner plate–size circle of bright light on the cloth.

2 To make the inside version, tape or tack the sheet across

why do bugs fly into lights?

Scientists aren't sure, but most agree that moths and other flying insects aren't actually attracted to light—they're confused by it. Some think that the insects use the Moon to navigate by, like sailors use stars, and that they mistake bright light for the Moon. A light from a bulb or camp-fire is a lot closer than the Moon, so when they try to follow the "moon" light they end up flying into the human-made light instead.

jumpers, creepers, and crawlers

Field cricket

All you have to do to find these buggy night creatures (and lots more) is look up, look down, listen all around.

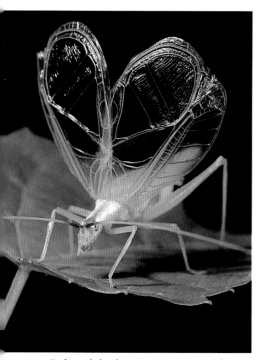

Rub-a-dub chrrrrrr. To sing, crickets such as this tree cricket raise their wings and rub the bases together.

CRICKETS

Crickets are lead singers in the symphony of night sounds. Only males sing, to call females and claim territory. They make the sound by raising their wings slightly and rubbing the bases together in a scissorslike motion. One wing's base is rough and the other is notched. To make your own cricket sounds in a similar way, run a thumbnail along the teeth of a comb over and over again. Chrrrrrrrr-up, chrrrrrrrr-up, chrrrrrrrr-up! Each kind of cricket makes its own special sound. Field crickets make clear, musical chirps one at a time. Ground crickets make a continuous trilling note by rubbing their wings back and forth 40 times a second. Most tree crickets sing chiming notes, like spring peeper frogs. Snowy tree crickets chirp softly (see The Thermometer Cricket).

the thermometer cricket

Snowy tree crickets are sometimes called "thermometer crickets" because their singing can tell you the temperature.

To find a snowy tree cricket, listen for a soft chirp, chirp, chirp in the trees. Although all tree crickets look a lot alike (see the photo, lower left), most make a constant chirrrrrrrrrring sound. The snowy is the only kind that makes individual chirp notes. (Ignore field crickets chirping on the ground. They're not reliable "thermometers.")

Found the right cricket? Okay, now look at your watch and count the number of chirps the snowy tree cricket makes in one minute. Divide that number by four, and add 40. Usually, the total is within a few degrees of the actual air temperature.

Listen to katydids on warm nights, then on cooler evenings. Like other calling insects, they sing faster and louder when the temperature is higher.

KATYDIDS

If you spot an insect that looks like a piece of thin green leaf turned edgeways with a grasshopper's legs and head attached, it's probably a katydid.

Katydids are main players in the nighttime insect band's rhythm section. From dusk till early morning all summer, you can hear the males high up in trees keeping a steady chirping beat: Katy-DID, katy-DID, katy-DID, katy-DID. Every once in a while, they'll throw in an extra beat: katy-DIDN'T. Like crickets, katydids sing by rubbing the bases of their wings together. In just one season,

a male katydid calls between 30 million and 50 million times. That's a lot of wing-rubbing. (Go ahead; see how many times you can rub your arms back and forth across each other before you get tired!)

GREEN LACEWINGS

These quiet, pale green insects have long antennae, bright gold- or copper-colored eyes, and lacy see-through wings up to 2 inches (5 cm) long. Like moths, they're attracted to light, so you'll probably see them if you try the light-and-sheet insect collector on page 97. Take a close look at their delicate, fairylike wings. Gardeners like green lacewings because their larvae eat aphids and other garden pests.

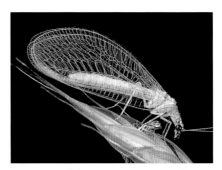

Peeyew-tiful. It's easy to see why this beautiful insect is called a green lacewing. But some kinds smell bad, so it's also known as a stink fly.

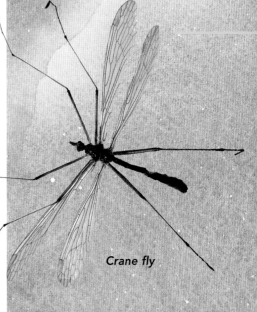

Crane fly

CRANE FLIES

Crane flies come flying softly to porch lights and window screens, bouncing up and down on their super-long legs. They look like giant mosquitoes. They're shaped the same as mosquitoes and have similar-looking legs and wings, but they're 20 times bigger. So many people think that crane flies must bite like mosquitoes that there's a special word for fear of them: tipulophobia. Actually, crane flies can't bite at all (whew!). They're completely harmless to humans.

JUNE BUGS

Plop! Flop! Bzzzz! At night, these big bumbling brownish bugs fly head-long into lighted porch walls and window screens and crash-land upside down on the ground, wings buzzing and legs waving in the air. Turn the June bug right-side up and in a few seconds off it goes again—sometimes right back into another wall or window (duh!). June bugs are members of the scarab beetle family. There are about 30,000 different kinds of scarab beetles worldwide. Over 1,300 kinds live in the United States. All of them are active mainly at night and are attracted by light. Maybe you'll bump into one at night—or one might bump into you!

Clumsy clowns of the insect world: June bugs buzz and bumble and bounce their way through the night.

Ridge runners: Most ground beetles, like this one, have hard, ridged wing covers. If you find one, look quick! The strong-legged insects run fast for cover.

GROUND BEETLES

There are at least 40,000 kinds of ground beetles in the world. Some scientists think there may be 40,000 more that haven't been dis-covered yet (maybe a new kind is living in *your* yard). During the day, ground beetles hide under leaves, stones, or tree bark. At night, they come out to hunt for small insect larvae. Almost all ground beetles are black or dark brown. They have powerful legs and can run fast. Some ground beetles are attracted to light or to sweet stuff such as moth "sugar" (page 89). Watch them, but don't pick them up. Some kinds give off a chemical that irritates skin.

what's a "bug"?

Most people use the word "bug" to mean any kind of insect. That's how the word is used in this book, too. To scientists, though, the word "bug" means only a particular group of insects, ones with special needle-like mouth parts made to suck up juices from plants or (yuck) animals. So be careful how you use the word "bug" around bug scientists, or you might bug them.

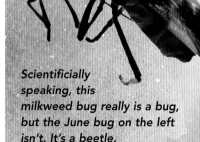

Scientificially speaking, this milkweed bug really is a bug, but the June bug on the left isn't. It's a beetle.

Quick, get back in the hole! Earthworms usually come out only at night. Too much sunlight can dry their moist skin.

EARTHWORMS

Earthworms aren't insects, of course—they're a special kind of animal, members of a family called *annelids*. But they come out at night and creep and crawl on the ground. So when you're looking for bugs after dark, look for earthworms, too.

There are actually more than 3,000 kinds of earthworms. Some are as small as an eyelash. In Australia, some kinds grow up to 10 feet (3 m) long! Most earthworms, though, including those that live in Europe and North America, are only between 2 and 6 inches (5 and 15.2 cm) long.

Sunlight can hurt earthworms, so they spend the day underground, eating their way through the soil and gobbling up leaves, bits of dead insects, and other food in their path. After dark, when the air is cool and moist, they come out of their burrows to breathe fresh air (earthworms breathe through their skin) and to drag more leafy food underground. Look for their long, glistening bodies on garden soil and among wet leaves. Or try "fiddling" for them (see Calling All Worms).

calling all worms

Earthworms can't see or hear, but they're sensitive to vibrations in the ground. For centuries people have used this fact to trick worms into coming to the surface. It's called "fiddling" or "calling" for worms. To try it one evening, pound a long, straight wooden stick or stake 1 to 2 feet (30.5 to 61 cm) deep into moist soil where you know worms live. Then rub the part of the stake still sticking out of the ground with a bumpy stick, or one with notches cut into it. Move the stick back and forth, the way a fiddler moves a bow over a violin's strings. The rubbing sends vibrations into the ground that resemble the vibrations moles make when they're digging for worms to eat. For a worm, that means danger, move out! After a few minutes of fiddling (and with a little luck), worms by the dozen will come squirming out of their holes.

bugs in a can

Beetles and other earth-bound night insects creep and crawl mostly out of sight, hidden beneath grass and leaves. To study them, make a simple trap.

what you need
Trowel
A large, wide-mouth container or can
2 bricks or rocks
A flat board bigger than the
   can's opening

what to do

1 Find a place with lots of grass or leaves, where bugs are likely to live.

2 Just before sunset, dig a hole and bury the can deep enough so that its open end is level with the ground. Pack the dirt around the can's edges right up to the rim. Ground beetles and other insects will fall into the trap and won't be able to crawl out.

3 Put a brick (or rock) on one side of the can and another on the opposite side.

4 Lay the board on the bricks so it forms a roof over the can's opening. The roof keeps rain out and stops birds from stealing the bugs you catch.

5 Check your trap in the morning. How many bugs are down there, and what kinds are they? Study them where they are (don't reach into the can because some beetles can bite) and use a field guide to help you identify them. When you're finished, pull the can out of the ground and let the insects go in a safe place, in leaves or under a bush. Remember to fill the hole with soil, too.

something else to try:
Put your trap in different kinds of places—in the woods, the garden, or at the edge of your lawn, for example. Do you find different insects in different places?

spiders

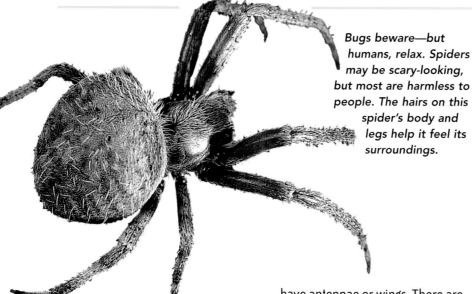

Bugs beware—but humans, relax. Spiders may be scary-looking, but most are harmless to people. The hairs on this spider's body and legs help it feel its surroundings.

Have you ever stepped outside early in the morning and walked face-first into a spider web? Eck! Where'd that web come from, anyway? It wasn't there the day before. Most spiders come out at night to build their webs or hunt. Not all kinds make webs, but most that do weave their traps under cover of darkness. Sometimes in the morning you can easily see their night's work because the webs are covered with dew and sparkle in the sun.

You probably know that spiders aren't actually insects— they're *arachnids*. Insects have antennae, wings, and six legs. Spiders have eight legs and don't have antennae or wings. There are between 30,000 and 50,000 kinds of spiders on our planet! Different kinds of web-weaving spiders build different-shaped webs. Some are flat, some are bowl shaped, some are triangular. House spiders build "cobwebs" that crisscross every which way. Orb weavers build round, crisscrossed webs, the kind most people think of. Funnel web spiders weave cavelike webs in grass and weeds. They wait inside the silky cave for a tasty insect to walk by, then run out, grab it, and drag their dinner inside (if spiders ran fast-food restaurants, you'd definitely want to *avoid* the drive-in windows).

A spider makes liquid silk inside glands in its

catch a spider web

If you find a web without a spider, you can bring the web home. First, lightly spray the web all over with white water-based spray paint. Then, while the paint is still wet, put a sheet of dark-colored foam-core board or construction paper behind the web and lift the paper until the web's silk anchor lines break. The web will stay on the paper and the paint will make it easy to see.

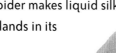

abdomen, then draws the silk out through faucetlike openings called *spinnerettes*. The silk turns solid as soon as it contacts air. A spider can make different sorts of silk for different purposes—sticky, dry, thick, thin, stretchy, stiff—depending on how it mixes and pulls out its silk-making

Webs are easiest to find in the morning, when they're covered in dew. Most spiders don't like wet webs, but this yellow garden spider decided to stay.

chemicals. Some spider silk is stronger, by weight, than steel.

When an insect is caught in a spider's web, the spider throws out a rope of silk to tie down the victim, or holds it with its front legs. Then the spider bites the insect and paralyzes the prey with a poison. To eat, spiders don't chew their food—they drink it. A spider injects its prey with a digestive juice that turns the bug's insides to liquid. Then it sucks up the goo and tosses the bug's body out of the web.

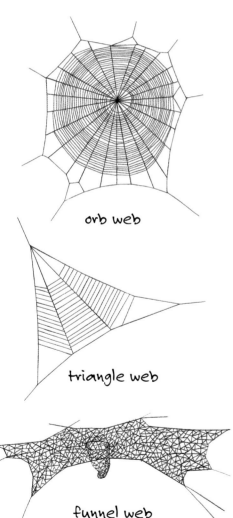

orb web

triangle web

funnel web

go on a spider hunt

Most spiders hide during the day. How many kinds can you find at night? Grab a flashlight and start looking. Shine the light on the ground in a garden, lawn, or among leaves. If two beady little green or golden eyes glitter back at you with eye shine, you've found a wolf spider prowling for a meal. Wolf spiders don't build webs; they run and catch prey like . . . well, like a wolf. Orb weavers build webs in bushes and near porch lights. If you don't bother them, they'll stay still and you can study them. Sketch the spiders in a notebook, or bring a camera and take photos of the spiders you find.

what's a bug's favorite color?

You've probably noticed bugs flying around street-lights at night. But do you suppose that night insects are attracted to just any color of light? Or are certain kinds attracted only to certain colors? Hmmm . . .

what you need

A warm, dark night

4 bright flashlights

1 piece each of blue, red, and yellow cellophane or plastic slightly larger than the flashlight lens

Tape or rubber bands

Notepad

Pencil

what to do

1. Make sure all the flashlights have strong batteries. Cover each of three of the flashlights' lenses with blue, red, or yellow cellophane or plastic (which you can buy at art and crafts stores). Fold the plastic over the lens and use tape or a rubber band to hold it in place. Or, if your flashlights have a removable ring that holds the lens, take the ring off, put the plastic over the lens, and screw the ring back down.

2. After dark on a warm, buggy night, set the four flashlights out in an open area at least 20 feet (6 m) apart and turn them on. Gradually insects will start coming to—which lights?

3. Sit by each color light for several minutes and watch carefully. How many insects are on or near the red light? The blue? The yellow? The white (uncolored)? Write down the numbers for each color in your notebook. Do different colors seem to attract different kinds of insects? Do you see crawling insects, such as beetles, as well as flying types? Write down descriptions of the insects you see for each color, or sketch them. Later, you can look them up in a field guide.

4. Visit each of the lights several times. If you see more or fewer insects, or new kinds, write down those observations, too.

5. Compare your observations to what scientists have observed. Some researchers think that moths are particularly drawn to blue light or bright white light. Yellow light doesn't seem to attract most insects but it helps humans to see—that's why yellow light bulbs are used on porches. Red light is almost invisible to many nocturnal insects and has the least effect. But what about *your* experiment? Do your results agree?

eyes to the sky

Under the cover of night? *Hidden by darkness?* It's true that night's darkness covers and hides the sights we're used to seeing in the daytime world. But night also *uncovers* sights we'd never see without darkness.

Just look at the dazzling night sky. The stars are always up there, day and night. We don't notice them during the day because our nearest star, the Sun, is so close and bright it outshines them.

Only the shadow of night uncovers the countless other stars sparkling in space. Only the shadow of night makes us turn our eyes to the sky, gaze at the far-off stars, and wonder: "What's out there?"

starry night

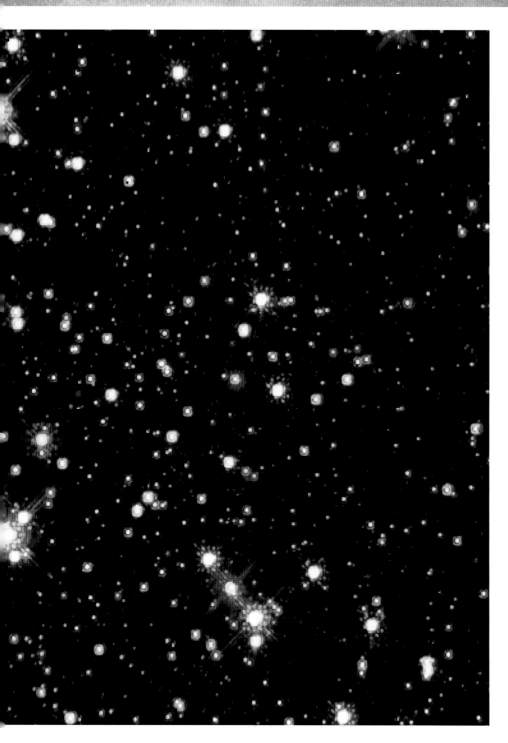

On a clear, dark night away from city lights, the sky twinkles and glitters with stars, planets, meteors, and more. Maybe someday you'll travel into space to get a closer look. But you can explore space from Earth, too, right now. Let's do it.

SKY-WATCHING BASICS

All you really need for stargazing, of course, are your own eyes and a dark night. Nothing could be simpler. Instructions: 1) Go outdoors. 2) Tilt your head back. 3) Watch the sky.

Even if this is all you ever do as a stargazer, you'll see some amazing sights: shooting stars, constellations, our moon, orbiting satellites, and more.

But there are ways to make stargazing even more interesting and fun. Here are some tips:

- Choose a dark place. The best place for stargazing is away from lights that make stars harder to see. If you live in the country away from lights, great. If you live in a town or city, find the darkest place in your yard, away from street and house lights.

- Choose a dark night. Nights when the Moon is full or nearly so are the worst times for stargazing. Moonless nights, or times before the Moon is up, are best.

- Pick an open area. Find a place where there are no nearby buildings and trees to block your view of the horizon (where the sky meets the earth in the distance). If you live in a city, a rooftop might be your best choice. Be sure it's safe, though, and ask a grownup to go with you.

- Have a seat, or lie down on your back. If you do all your sky watching while standing, you'll give yourself a . . . errrk, ouch . . . stiff neck. Use a chair or spread a blanket on the ground and make yourself comfortable.

- Let your eyes adjust. Remember, it takes 15 to 45 minutes for your eyes to see their best in darkness (see Tips for Better Night Eyes on page 24). Give them time to adjust. And if you bring a flashlight, cover its lens with red plastic so the light won't ruin your night vision.

- Boost your eye power with binoculars. Serious amateur astronomers use high-quality telescopes to view distant star formations. But a good telescope is expensive. When you're just starting out, binoculars are a better choice. There's nothing wimpy about good binoculars for stargazing. They'll help you see a lot more in the night sky. At least two comets have been discovered by amateurs using binoculars!

Binoculars come in different models described with numbers such as 7 x 35 or 8 x 40. The first number tells you how many times larger something looks with the binoculars than without. The second number tells you how big the lenses are. Larger lenses gather more light and let you see fainter

stars. For beginning astronomers, binocular models such as 8 x 40 or 7 x 50 are good choices and are also handy for daytime wildlife watching.

- Learn what to watch for. The next few pages show you some of the sights to look for in the night sky. But it's a big universe out there, with a lot for a star-gazing Earthling to learn. Plus, objects in the sky are constantly changing positions because the Earth is constantly rotating. So you need to learn not only *what* to watch for, but *where and when* to watch for it. How? Astronomy books and computer programs include star charts that show the positions of the stars in the sky at different times and seasons and are a great way to get to know the night sky. So is visiting a planetarium, or joining an astronomy club. Most important, spend some "sky time" finding one or two special stars or constellations each night. Soon you'll be an expert.

How far does space go? Nobody really knows. There are billions of stars in our galaxy, and billions of other galaxies.

is someone looking back at you?

You're standing there gazing at a far-off twinkling star . . . hmmm, what's that odd feeling . . . as if someone (or something) is looking back at you? Are there other forms of life out there?

Most astronomers believe the answer is probably yes. Why? Because there are so many possible worlds out there. Scientists calculate that at least 40 billion stars, or one out of every 10, in the Milky Way galaxy are similar in size and temperature to our sun. Of those, at least one billion are likely to have orbiting planets, and of those planets, some say, the odds are that somewhere between ten thousand and one million could support intelligent life.

Now add the 100 billion or more other galaxies in the universe, and . . . well, maybe you'd better make sure you're dressed nicely the next time you go stargazing. There may be a whole crowd of alien creatures looking back at you.

great galaxy!

Star-filled pinwheel: The Milky Way is a spiral galaxy, one of many like this galaxy photographed in deep space by the Hubble Space Telescope.

As you look at the night sky, nearly every star you see is a part of our home galaxy, the Milky Way galaxy, a flat, swirling pinwheel of gases, space dust, and stars—*billions* of them.

Every star in the galaxy is a sun. Our sun is our closest star. It's "only" 93 million miles from Earth. Our next-nearest star (Proxima Centauri) is 25 *trillion* miles from Earth. If the thickness of this page stood for the distance from our sun to Earth, the distance from our next-nearest star

to Earth would be a stack of paper 71 feet tall. Light from our sun takes eight minutes to reach us. The Milky Way galaxy is so big, it would take 100,000 *years* for light from a sun at one end of the galaxy to reach the other end.

How many stars are out there? Most scientists now think there are approximately 400 billion. Some think there may be as many as one thousand billion—in other words, one *trillion* stars. And that's just in

our galaxy. The Milky Way galaxy is only one of at least 100 billion galaxies that make up our universe.

It's a good thing our eyes can't see all the stars in our galaxy at once, or we'd be so dazzled we'd never get any sleep. Most are too distant to see without a super-powerful telescope. On a clear, dark night away from lights, you can see about 2,000 to 3,000 stars. Most stars glow white or

Viewed from its side, this far-off spiral galaxy resembles a thick band of stars.

yellowish white, but others are pale red, blue, or gold. Different stars are different sizes and distances from Earth, so some look dim to us and some look bright.

Our sun and its nine planets are about halfway toward the outer edge of the Milky Way galaxy. Stars are clustered more closely together at the galaxy's center. At the outside edges, great "arms" of stars spiral outward, like pinwheel fireworks or water spinning from a rotating lawn sprinkler.

From our view on Earth, we gaze edgewise across and through our flat, spinning galaxy. The star-filled center resembles a wide, white band across the sky: the "milk" in the Milky Way.

how much is one billion?

One billion galaxies. One trillion stars: Astronomers use numbers so big they're hard to imagine. Exactly how much is one billion (1,000,000,000)? How much is one trillion (1,000,000,000,000)?

Picture yourself counting out loud: one, two, three . . . one number every second.

To count to one million (1,000,000), you'd have to count nonstop, day and night, for 11 ½ days.

To count to one billion, you'd have to stay awake counting every second for almost 32 years. (Are you sleepy yet?)

And to count to one trillion, you'd have to . . . well, you'd have to forget it. It would take at least 31,688 years.

super stars

Like trying to find just a few particular marbles out of 3,000 scattered all over your bedroom floor—that's the feeling you might get when you first try to figure out what's what in the star-filled night sky. Fortunately, there are a few standout stars and groups of stars that can help you find your way around.

If you live in the United States or anywhere else in the Northern Hemisphere, you probably already know at least one standout star group, the Big Dipper, which looks just like its name. Its big bowl and long, curving handle are easy to spot.

Once you've found the Big Dipper you can use it to point your way to Polaris, the North Star. See the two bright stars that form the front of the dipper's bowl? The star at the bowl's bottom is Merak; at the top is Dubhe. To find Polaris, draw an imaginary line from Merak to Dubhe and then straight out about five times longer until you come to a medium bright star all by itself: Polaris, the star that always points north. You're looking at the same star that Christopher Columbus and other famous explorers used to guide them to new lands.

When you find Polaris you've also found the Little Dipper. Polaris is at the tip of the Little Dipper's handle. The Big and Little Dippers are always positioned so that when one is right side up the other is upside down, with their handles facing in opposite directions.

The Big Dipper also points to another special star. If you follow the curve of its handle away from the bowl, you'll come to Arcturus, a beautiful orange star that's 25 times bigger than our sun and one of the brightest in the night sky.

polaris

little dipper

dubhe   merak

alcor   mizar

big dipper

to arcturus

meet mizar and alcor

Look at the next-to-last star in the Big Dipper's handle. Now look again. Do you see two stars, one larger than the other? The biggest is called Mizar and the small, faint star next to it is Alcor. If you don't look carefully, they seem like a single star. (Actually, they're not near each other at all, but they're in the same line of view from Earth, so they seem close. Such stars are called optical doubles.) Before there were eye charts, Alcor was used to test vision—if you couldn't see it, you didn't have good eyesight. The star was even called "The Test" in some cultures.

PICTURES IN THE SKY

To help them find their way around the night sky, ancient stargazers divided the sky into 88 groups of stars, called constellations, that form imaginary patterns or figures. If you've ever played connect-the-dots you get the idea. The Big Dipper is part of the constellation Ursus Major, or the Big Bear, because the dipper's handle and bowl reminded the ancients of a bear's tail and body. The Little Dipper forms the constellation Ursus Minor, or the Little Bear. Other constellations include the Swan, the Archer, and the Crab.

Because Earth is rotating, all the stars and constellations seem to rotate around Polaris. The stars closest to Polaris turn small circles and are always visible at night. Stars farther from Polaris turn larger circles, so they're not always visible above the horizon.

The constellations that always shine above the horizon are called *circumpolar* constellations. The six circumpolar constellations visible from North America include Ursus Major, Ursus Minor, and the four shown on this page.

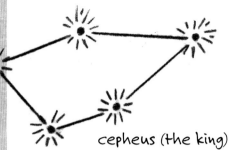

cepheus (the king)

cepheus (the king)

If you stretch the imaginary line you drew between the Big Dipper and the North Star even farther, past Polaris, you'll come to the peak of this house-shaped constellation's "roof." The King's stars aren't very bright, so look carefully.

cassiopea (the queen)

cassiopea (the queen)

The Queen lives right next door to the King. Sometimes it looks like an "M" and sometimes like a "W," but it's always bright and easy to find.

draco (the dragon)

The Dragon is a string of faint stars that stretches all the way from the tip of its tail above the Big Dipper's bowl to its four-star head that looks like a dim "Even Littler Dipper."

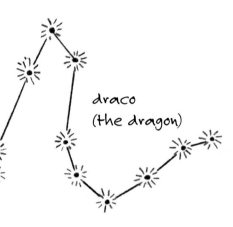

draco
(the dragon)

camelopardalis (the giraffe)

This constellation is not only hard to pronounce (kam-uh-lo-PAR-duh-lis)—it's also hard to see, because its stars are so dim. On a very dark night, you can sometimes make out its scraggly legs and neck near Cassiopea.

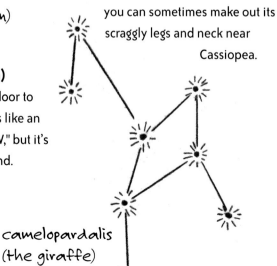

camelopardalis
(the giraffe)

114

another starry signpost: orion (the hunter)

Orion isn't circumpolar, but it's visible in both the Northern and Southern Hemispheres from late fall to early spring and is an especially good sky marker.

Orion is easy to find because it has more bright stars than any other constellation. The star Betelgeuse (pronounced "beetle juice") forms one "shoulder" and is deep red.

Rigel, a "foot," is the seventh brightest star in the sky.

Orion's three-stars-in-a-row belt makes a handy pointer. Trace an imaginary line straight through it and extend the line on both sides. Follow the line on one side and you'll find Sirius, the brightest star in the sky, in Canis Major (The Big Dog constellation). Follow the line on the other side to Aldebran, a brilliant "red giant" star in Taurus (The Bull).

orion (the hunter)

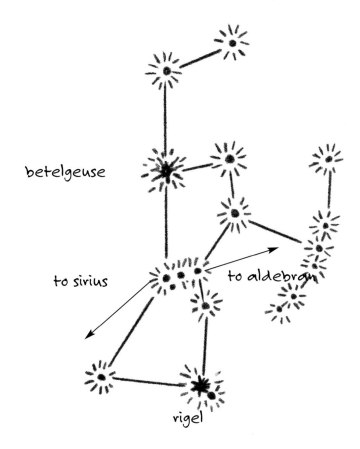

betelgeuse

to sirius

to aldebran

rigel

make your own constellations

If you have a hard time seeing the connect-the-stars lion picture in Leo, the scorpion in Scorpius, or the Hercules in Hercules, don't worry. You're not alone. Different people from different cultures see different pictures in the same star patterns. What people in North America call the Big Dipper, for instance, is known as The Plough in Great Britain and The Chariot in France.

You can put yourself in the place of the ancients from long ago and make up your own connect-the-dots constellations from stars in the night sky. When the ancients created constellation pictures, they chose their culture's favorite animals and heroes. What pictures do you see in star groups? A car, a computer, a skateboard? Just imagine a line tracing one star to the next to the next to the . . . hey, is that Bart Simpson up there?

star or planet?

On any night, at least one of the five closest planets—Mercury, Venus, Mars, Jupiter, Saturn— is visible in the sky without a telescope. As you gaze at the night sky, how can you tell whether you're looking at a planet— or just another star?

Most stars are enormous and produce huge amounts of energy and light. But they're also very far away. Our nearest star, after the Sun, is (gasp!) "only" 25 trillion (25,000,000,000,000) miles (40,230,000,000,000 km) from Earth! So we see stars only as tiny pinpoints. As the light

from a star passes through Earth's atmosphere, air movements make it shake and quiver. That's why stars seem to twinkle.

The planets are much smaller than stars, but they're also much closer to Earth. In telescopes, we see them as small circles, or discs, rather than pinpoints. And they usually don't twinkle. Instead, they shine steadily with light reflected from our sun.

So if you see a "star" in the night sky that's not twinkling, take a closer look. It's probably a planet.

Another important difference: Stars circle the sky together, keeping their positions. Planets wander across the night sky through a wide band of twelve constella- tions known together as the zodiac (the word "planet" is Greek for "a wan- derer.") Aries, Taurus, Gemini, Cancer, Leo, Virgo, Libra, Scorpius, Sagittarius,

Capricorn, Aquarius, and Pisces are the zodiac constellations. Over the weeks and months, as each planet orbits the Sun, it moves at its own speed from one constellation to another, changing its position in the sky compared to the stars and to the other planets. On any given evening a particular planet may be visible lower or higher in the sky, all night or part of the night or not at all. So where in the night sky do you look for a planet?

Fortunately, the movements and appearances of the planets are predictable. Astronomy magazines and websites provide charts that tell you what planets you can see each day and when and where you can see them.

there's no place like home

You're a space explorer returning from a long trip to a distant galaxy far beyond the Milky Way. Suddenly, up ahead, you see a huge ball covered in whirling, multicolored clouds. "Ah, Jupiter," you think as you zoom by. "We're almost home."

Of all the trillions of stars in space, only one—our sun—is circled by the nine special planets that make up our solar system. Each planet is an entirely different world. Each orbits the Sun at its own speed. Together, they're our home in the galaxy.

MERCURY

Distance from Sun: 35,983,000 miles (57,909,000 km)

Mercury is the closest planet to the Sun and is only slightly larger than our moon. Its surface is covered with craters created by crashing comets and meteors. Mercury zips around the Sun four times faster than Earth— its year is only 88 Earth days long. But it takes 59 Earth days for it to rotate just once on its axis. As Mercury slowly turns, the temperature on its sunny side sizzles to 800°F (427°C). Meanwhile, its night side shivers at 300°F below zero (-184°C). Brrrrr!

VENUS

Distance from Sun: 67,200,000 miles (108,208,930 km)

Venus, second closest to the Sun, is Earth's nearest next-door neighbor and one of the easiest planets to see. Other than the Sun and the Moon, it's the brightest object in our night sky. If you see an especially bright "star" in the west just after sunset or in the east just before sunrise, it's probably actually Venus. Venus is nice to look at, but you wouldn't want to live there. Thick clouds of carbon dioxide trap the Sun's heat, keeping the temperature at a toasty 800°F (427°C) while drizzling a constant rain of sulfuric acid. Does anybody have an extra-thick air-conditioned umbrella?

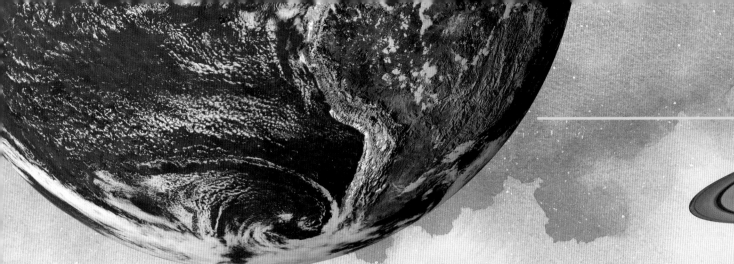

EARTH

Distance from Sun: 93,000,000 miles (150,000,000 km)

You already know where Earth is—right beneath your feet! But it's Earth's position in the solar system, and especially its distance from the Sun, that's the secret to its success as a place that supports life. Earth has an atmosphere that shields the planet from dangerous solar rays but lets in just the right amount of heat to keep temperatures comfortable and allow water to exist on the surface. Other planets are either too close (and too hot) for liquid water or too far (and too cold). But Earth? It's just right. Some scientists call the secret of Earth's life "The Goldilocks Principle."

MARS

Distance from Sun: 141,486,200 miles (227,700,000 km)

Mars shines blood red in the night sky. That's why the Romans named it after their god of war. Actually, the color is caused by oxide rust on the planet's dry, barren surface. Mars is half the size of Earth and has four distinct seasons. But instead of rain, snow, or sun, the changing seasons bring huge dust storms that cover the entire planet. There's enough frozen water at the Martian poles to flood the planet 100 feet deep (30.5 m) if it melted—but it won't. Mars is just too cold. Temperatures are as low as minus 190°F (-123°C).

JUPITER

Distance from Sun: 484,000,000 miles (778,412,010 km)

Jupiter, our largest planet, is a whopping 88,846 miles (142,984 km) across but has no solid surface. The planet is a huge ball of gas covered in a 600-mile-deep (965.6 km) blanket of swirling gas clouds. The clouds are what you see when you look at Jupiter shining in the night sky. The planet weighs more than all eight other planets combined! Its Great Red Spot, visible in a telescope or strong binoculars, is a 300-year-old storm bigger than two Earths. Jupiter also has 17 moons.

SATURN

Distance from Sun: 887,000,000 miles (1,426,725,400 km)

Saturn, the second largest planet in our solar system, also appears bright in the night sky. You'll need a telescope, though, to get a really good view of its famous multicolored rings, which are actually bands of ice particles—some tiny, some as big as houses. Like Jupiter, Saturn is a gas planet. Made mostly of liquid hydrogen and helium, it's covered in thick clouds of ammonia that swirl violently in storms with winds as strong as 1,000 miles (1,600 km) per hour.

Saturn has at least 30 moons.

URANUS

Distance from Sun: 1,780,000,000 miles (2,870,972,200 km)

Uranus, also a gas planet, is covered in a thick layer of methane gas that gives it a bluish green color. Its temperature is super cold: minus 320°F (-195°C)! Uranus may be our weirdest planet, because it spins on its side. Scientists think Uranus was knocked sideways by an enormous collision long ago. Now it revolves around the Sun spinning like a tipped-over top. Debris from the collision probably created at least some of its 21 moons.

NEPTUNE

Distance from Sun: 2,800,000,000 (4,498,252,900 km)

Neptune is the windiest planet in our solar system, with gusts up to 1,200 miles (1,931 km) per hour—that's twelve times more powerful than an Earth hurricane. Like the other gas planets it has no solid surface. Its swirling, wind-whipped atmosphere is mostly hydrogen and helium. Triton, one of Neptune's eight moons, is the coldest place in the solar system, with temperatures as low as minus 391°F (-235°C). Its huge geysers throw clouds of nitrogen gas as high as five miles (8 km).

PLUTO

Distance from Sun: 3,670,000,000 miles (5,906,376,200 km)

Pluto is definitely our smallest planet—it's only two-thirds the size of Earth's moon. Usually it's also our most distant planet. But its 248-year orbit around the Sun is lopsided instead of circular like the orbits of the other planets. For 20 of those years, it comes closer to the Sun than Neptune and becomes the eighth planet in our solar system. Pluto was the eighth planet from 1979 to 1999. Now it's the ninth planet again. There isn't a picture of Pluto here because it's so small and far away that scientists haven't been able to photograph it yet.

what is that in the sky?

Shooting stars, or meteors, are common sights in the night sky and last only a few seconds. Comets, such as Comet Hale-Bopp shown here, are huge balls of ice, rock, and gas that travel millions of miles. We see them only when their orbits bring them close to our sun.

Not everything high in the night sky is a star or planet. You don't have to stargaze long before you notice there are other things moving up there. What are they? Did you just see a flying saucer?

If the object flashes lights on and off as it moves steadily across the sky, it's probably an airplane. At night, an airplane is difficult to see except for its blinking lights, which are usually red or white. Listen carefully, and you might hear its engine.

Of course, you see airplanes all the time. So they might not seem as interesting to you as two other com-mon—and exciting—night-sky sights: shooting stars and satellites.

SHOOTING STARS

Suddenly a bright streak of light flashes through the sky and disappears. That's a shooting star— not really a star at all, but a *meteor*. A meteor is the light you see when a *meteoroid* enters Earth's atmosphere and burns up. Meteoroids are bits of rocky space debris. Most are about the size of a grain of sand and are dust left over from the creation of the solar system or from passing comets. Some are pea-size. A few are as big as baseballs or larger and are chunks broken off asteroids or planets.

There is no air in space. But when a meteoroid enters Earth's thick atmosphere 60 miles (96.6 km) above the surface it slams into air molecules while traveling as fast as 30,000 miles (48,280 km) per hour. At that speed, air pressure and friction make the meteoroid glow white hot. We see it as a streak of light: another meteor!

The best time to look for shooting stars is usually between midnight and dawn. On an average night, you can see about one meteor every 10 or 15 minutes. On certain nights of the year Earth passes through bands of meteoroids left from passing comets and a *meteor shower* happens. In some meteor showers you might see a meteor (or two) every minute! See the chart for the dates of major meteor showers.

Sometimes an especially large piece of debris doesn't burn up completely and reaches Earth. These are called *meteorites*. Large meteorites can create craters just like those on the Moon. Really big meteorites sometimes explode just above the surface. That's what happened in Siberia in 1908, when a massive meteorite exploded and destroyed a vast area of remote forest. About 30,000 years ago an even larger meteorite smashed into what is now Arizona in the United States and blew out a crater 570 feet (174 m) deep and 4,000 feet (1.2 km) wide.

MAJOR ANNUAL METEOR SHOWERS

Shower Name	Estimated Peak Date
Quadrantids	January 3–4
Lyrids	April 21
Eta Aquarids	May 4–5
Delta Aquarids	July 28–29
Perseids	August 12
Orionids	October 21
Leonids	November 16
Geminids	December 13
Ursids	December 22

duck! here comes a meteorite!

About one dozen meteorites crash-land on Earth every day. Most splash into the ocean. Of those that strike dry land, only a few are ever found. Some, though, make spectacular entrances.

In 1954 Ann Hodges, a housewife in the southern United States, was resting on her couch when an eight-pound (3.6 kg) meteorite crashed through her roof and struck her, bruising her hip.

In 1994 Jose Martin was driving a car near Madrid, Spain, when a three-pound (1.4 kg) meteorite smashed through his windshield and bounced into the backseat.

And in 2002 a 14-year-old English girl was getting into her family car when a walnut-size meteorite landed (softly) on her foot.

No need to worry about your safety, though: the odds of being struck by a meteorite are 1 in 10 trillion!

Many satellites, such as this MightySat I, are used for scientific research.

SOARING SATELLITES

There are almost 10,000 satellites orbiting Earth. Many are too high or too small for you to spot without a telescope. But hundreds are big enough and low enough for you to see as they cross the sky 100 to 500 miles (161 to 805 km) above. If you know where and when to look (astronomy magazines and websites tell you), you can even watch the International Space Station.

The best times to watch for satellites are the hour just after sunset and the hour just before sunrise. That's when we're in darkness but satellites high in the sky are still reflecting sunlight. It's the Sun's reflection that makes them visible. Satellites passing overhead in the middle of the night are in Earth's shadow and can't be seen.

How do you know if you're looking at a satellite? Satellites don't make a sound as they glide across the sky. And they don't blink steadily on and off, like a plane's lights. Satellites look like moving, shining stars. Some are brighter than others. Some flash briefly, then fade. Some twinkle slightly as they tumble in space. But satellites don't have blinking lights.

Most satellites are used to send communication signals—radio, TV, and telephone. Others are used for scientific research. And some are military spy satellites! When you spot a satellite, try to figure out the direction it's moving. Most American communication satellites move from west to east. Russian satellites and most military satellites travel from north to south or south to north. Maybe one of those satellites is looking back at *you*.

There are so many satellites orbiting Earth you'll almost certainly see one crossing the sky just after sunset. You might even spot the International Space Station, shown here.

moon watching

It's our nearest neighbor in the universe, and the only place other than Earth where humans have set foot. It's where the Man in the Moon lives. It's what makes werewolves come out at night. It's made of green cheese . . . whoa, wait a minute. Let's not get fiction mixed up with fact! (Obviously, only the first sentence is true.)

When it comes to the Moon, fact is just as amazing as fiction. For instance, we know that our moon has the power to make our planet's oceans rise and fall, producing the tides. As it orbits Earth, its gravity pulls on the ocean's waters, creating a bulge of higher water (high tide) where the Moon is overhead and lower water (low tide) on the sides. As Earth rotates, the tides move across the oceans.

Where did the Moon come from? Scientists aren't sure. But most now think the Moon was created when a Mars-size object crashed into a just-forming Earth 4.6 billion (4,600,000,000) years ago. The debris from that huge collision was blown into orbit around our future planet and came together to form the Moon. At first the Moon's surface was super hot and molten, like lava.

As it cooled, the lunar crust formed. Over time, impacts from crashing meteorites created its many craters and pounded the surface into a thick layer of powdery rock dust called the *regolith*.

The Moon isn't at all like Earth. It has no liquid water, no weather, and no breathable air. When the Sun is up, the temperature on the surface sizzles to 243°F (117°C); at night, it's *minus* 272°F (-169°C). And the Moon is much smaller than Earth: just 2,159 miles (3,475 km) across. That's only about two-thirds as wide as the United States. Picture a basketball as the size of Earth. The Moon would be a tennis ball.

Even though it's little, the Moon is easy to see because it's so close: just 238,855 miles (384,400 km) from Earth, more than 10 times closer than our nearest planet, Venus. Use binoculars to see the moon's craters and mountains, or use a telescope to get an even better look. Surprisingly, the best time to watch the Moon is *not* when the Moon is full. The Sun's bright reflection on the full moon's surface hides craters and mountains. Instead, do your moon watching anytime when the Moon *isn't* full.

GETTING TO KNOW THE MOON

Of course, unless you're a tiny baby (congratulations on your early reading skills), you're already familiar with the Moon. After all, you've seen it almost every day of your life. But you can learn a lot more about the Moon by looking just a little more carefully.

Even without binoculars or a telescope you can clearly see light and dark areas on the Moon's surface. Galileo and other early astronomers thought the dark areas were oceans, like those on Earth, and called them *maria*, the Latin word for seas. We still call them seas—but now we know they're actually flat, dried lava beds, where lava filled in the bottoms of craters. When you look at the Moon and see a "face" (see page 127), the eyes and mouth are old lava beds.

Early astronomers thought the Moon's light areas were continents and called them *terrae* for "land." Today we call those places the lunar *highlands*. They're packed with overlapping meteorite craters. When you look at the Moon's light areas you're looking at craters on top of craters on top of craters.

Have you noticed that whenever you look at the Moon it's always facing the same way? That's because the Moon rotates on its axis at exactly the same speed that it orbits Earth (once every 27 days, 7 hours, and 43 minutes, to be exact). So getting to know the Moon is one-sided. The far side is never visible.

Binoculars will give you a better look at the Moon's features and reveal some of its craters. You'll need a telescope to look closely enough to make out most of the lunar landmarks in the photo here. If you don't have binoculars or a telescope, just use the photo to help you guess where these landmarks are in the Moon's light and dark areas.

apollo landing sites

Between 1969 and 1972, six Apollo moon missions landed on the Moon at the sites shown here. All together 12 astronauts explored the surface of the Moon and brought back 840 pounds (381 kg) of moon rocks for scientists to study. No human has visited the moon since—but someday scientists and astronauts will live there at a permanent base. At the Apollo 15, 16, and 17 landing sites, moon buggies left behind by the astronauts are waiting for the next visitors to take them for a ride. Maybe you'll be one of them!

sea of tranquility

Like other dark areas, the Sea of Tranquility isn't a sea but an enormous, flat lava bed formed when lava oozed from beneath the surface after an enormous impact with an asteroid or meteorite. The first humans to walk on the Moon touched down at the western edge of the Sea of Tranquility and announced: "Houston, Tranquility Base here. The Eagle has landed."

tycho

Bright streaks, or rays, stretch out in all directions from large craters such as Tycho. They were created by debris blown out when the crater formed. Tycho is 53 miles (85 km) wide. Its walls are two miles (3.2 miles km) high!

copernicus

Copernicus is another massive impact crater, 56 miles across (90 km). One of its long rays crosses the site where Apollo 12 landed.

kepler

This crater is about 300 miles (482.8 km) to the left of Copernicus and is 20 miles (32.2 km) across, with lots of rays extending outward.

aristarchus

Aristarchus is another especially big crater, 26 miles (42 km) across. Like other craters more than 24 miles (40 km) wide, the impact that created it left mountains in the center from debris that splashed upward, the way a raindrop splashes upward when it strikes the ground.

your name here?

Many of the Moon's areas are named for famous astronomers and other scientists who've made exciting discoveries about our nearest neighbor. Someday, will there be a place up there with *your* name on it?

the moon and its phases

Moon Phases

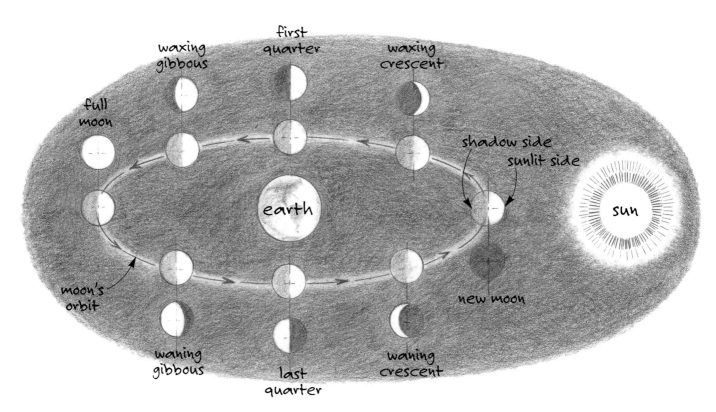

waxing gibbous

first quarter

waxing crescent

full moon

shadow side
sunlit side

earth

sun

moon's orbit

new moon

waning gibbous

last quarter

waning crescent

Half of the Moon is always facing the Sun and half is always in shadow. From Earth, we can never see the shadowy part in the blackness of space. How much of the sunlit side we can see depends on where the Moon is in its orbit around us. We call our changing views of the Moon's sunlit side its "phases."

The photo of the Moon on page 125 shows a big round disc—a full moon. But as you know, the Moon doesn't always look round to us. Sometimes it's a thin curve, or crescent. Sometimes it's a half moon. Sometimes it's not visible at all. We call these changes in the Moon's appearance *phases*. But they're really just changes in our view of the Moon's shiny side as it orbits Earth.

As the Moon circles us, one half is always lit by the Sun and the other half is always dark. On Earth, we can't see the dark part. But we can see the sunlit part. How *much* of the sunlit part we can see depends on where the Moon is in its orbit.

When the Moon is between the Earth and Sun, its sunlit side is pointing away from us. We can't see its dark side against the dark sky, so we can't see the Moon at all. We call that a *new moon*, but a better name might be "no moon."

As the Moon continues to revolve around Earth, we can see a little more of the sunlight striking it each day: First, we see just a sliver (a *crescent* moon), then half (a *first quarter* moon), then all but a sliver (a *gibbous* moon). Two weeks later, when the Moon is halfway around its orbit, its entire sunny side is facing us. We can see a big, bright disc: *full moon*. During this whole time, when we're seeing more and more of the Moon's bright side, we say it's *waxing*.

After the full moon, we start seeing less and less of the Moon's lit side. We say it's *waning*. Gradually, it moves back through gibbous, last quarter, and crescent phases, and then vanishes again: *no moon* (um, *new* moon).

The Moon takes about 29 days to complete its cycle of phases. The next time you see the Moon, try to figure out which phase it's in and whether it's waxing or waning.

pictures in the moon

What do you see when you look at the Moon? All over the world, people from different cultures see different pictures in the full moon's light and dark areas. It all depends on where you grew up and the stories you heard about the Moon.

If you live in the United States, you probably see the entire Moon as a face that you call "The Man in the Moon." Dark areas (highlighted in the drawing below) form its two eyes, nose, and mouth.

But in Europe, "The Man in the Moon" most people see is a whole person carrying a bundle of sticks on his back.

In other parts of the world people see a rabbit, a toad, a crab, and other animals and shapes in the Moon. Try to see these other shapes when you look at the Moon. Or make up some of your own. Hmmm . . . doesn't that fuzzy patch look a lot like Uncle Fred's moustache? And there's his big nose, and . . .

Man in the Moon face

Man carrying bundle of sticks

how to shrink the moon

Have you ever noticed that when the Moon is just above the horizon (where the ground meets the sky) it looks bigger than usual? Sometimes it looks gigantic. How can that be? After all, it's the Moon, not a balloon. It can't expand or shrink. The Moon is always the same size and distance from Earth, no matter whether it's high or low in the sky. If you take a photo of the "giant" moon with a camera, the moon in the picture looks normal size.

So why does the Moon sometimes *look* way huge to us?

Scientists have been scratching their heads over that question for centuries. They still don't all agree on *why* a low moon seems extra big. But they do know that it's an optical illusion. In other words, our brains are playing tricks on us.

Most scientists think the illusion has something to do with the way your brain compares the sizes of objects in your line of sight and the distances between you and them, and figures out their actual size. For instance, when you see a car that's far away and small looking, your brain doesn't tell you that you're looking at a tiny toy car. It compensates for the distance so you're aware that you're looking at a normal-size car. When you look at the Moon close to the horizon, the trees and houses and other objects between you and the Moon get in your brain's way. They make it obvious that the Moon is very far away— so far that your brain tries to make up for it too much by making the Moon look bigger.

The illusion is hard to understand, even for scientists. But it's fun to think about— and even more fun to undo. You can shrink that seemingly huge moon back to normal size.

All you have to do is block out the land and objects your brain sees between you and the Moon. Try holding your hand out just beneath the Moon so that it hides the horizon. Or "pinch" the moon between your thumb and forefinger—or look at it through a cardboard tube from a roll of paper towels. And here's a really weird way to shrink the moon: Look at it while standing on your head! Presto—the Moon pops back to actual size.

make a moon catcher

Scatter moonbeams around your room with this sparkling mobile. You can string the shiny dangles any way you want, with big and little charms and homemade beads in different shapes.

what you need

2 pieces of wood dowel rod, 3/16-inch (5 mm) diameter and 9 to 10 inches (22.9 to 25.4 cm) long

Silver paint

Paintbrush

Black yarn

Scissors

Shiny mirror paper (sold in craft stores)

Glue stick

Pencil

Monofilament fishing line

Assorted clear and reflective beads

Silver star-shaped buttons or charms

Aluminum foil

Toothpick

Small wire hooks (or bendable wire)

what to do

1 First you'll make the frame that will hold your mobile's moon and dangling beads and charms. Start by painting the two dowels with silver paint. Then let them dry completely.

2 Cross the two dowels, one centered over the other, and lash them together where they cross by wrapping and tying them with yarn. Then tie one end of a long piece of yarn around the center of the lashed dowels, hold the other end up, and cut it off where it measures 10 inches (25.4 cm) above the sticks.

3 Cut two pieces of yarn 6 inches (15.2 cm) longer than the dowels. Tie the ends of one piece to the ends of one of the dowels, then do the same with the other yarn and dowel. Gather the two cross pieces of yarn where they meet in the middle and wrap the center strand of yarn around them and up. Make a loop at the end of the center strand

for hanging the mobile. When you hold the frame up by the center yarn loop, it should hang straight and level.

4 Now you're ready to make the mobile's moonbeam-catching decorations. To create the center moon, put two pieces of shiny mirror paper back to back, with the white sides facing in and the shiny sides out. Cut out a moon shape about 6 inches (15.2 cm) tall. Glue the two pieces together with glue stick so the moon is shiny on both sides. Poke a hole in one end of the moon and, using a short piece of fishing line, hang it from the frame's center.

5 Now make eight strands of beads, buttons, and charms in different combinations and lengths, from 8 to 14 inches (20.3 to 35.6 cm) long. Just string and tie whatever combinations of decorations you want onto fishing line. Crumple or roll aluminum foil around a tooth-pick, then take the toothpick out, to make your own reflective balls and cylinders, each with a central hole for stringing. Tie knots wherever you

need to keep the decorations from slipping, and make a loop at one end of each strand for hanging.

6 Use small wire hooks to hang the strands, or make your own from bendable wire. Slip one end of a hook over the frame, then hang a strand from the hook's other end.

7 You'll have to experiment a while with the spacing and positions of the beaded strands to get the mobile to balance evenly. When you succeed, hang your sparkling moon catcher in a window or outdoors where it will reflect moonlight.

the edges of night

We call them *dawn* and *dusk*. They're the in-between times, when night is on its way to day or vice versa. The sky is tinged in soft pink or aflame with red-orange as the sun rises or sets. The air is cool and moist. Morning's dawn and evening's dusk are times of change. Flowers open or close. Breezes pick up or die down. Often, they're the best times for watching wildlife. Night *and* day creatures are out and about, one shift headed for bed and the other starting to search for food or a mate.

Like the night itself, the edges of night are great places to explore.

good morning!

What's the first thing you hear when you wake up in the morning? Probably birds singing. Even in cities, morning birds tweet and chirp over the sounds of cars and horns and trains and planes. For a bird, dawn begins about an hour before yours does, because birds' eyes have more rods (see page 12) and are more sensitive to the just-rising Sun's dim light.

The birds you hear singing first thing in the morning are males. Different kinds sing different songs, but they're all saying mostly the same thing: "Here I am! This is my place!" Male birds sing to stake out territory and to invite possible mates to fly by

for a closer look. Mornings are especially full of birdsong in spring and summer, when birds are nesting and starting families. Some songbirds sing a whole variety of songs—like singers at a concert. Male song sparrows have a repertoire of 10 songs, and they sing each one several times before switching to the next.

Both male and female birds also make other sounds, known as *calls*. Calls are usually short and simple and less musical than songs. Birds use them to "talk" to each other, to warn of danger or tell others they've found food. A northern cardinal's pretty song sounds like *purdy, purdy, purdy*. But its call is a serious-sounding *chit! chit! chit!*

Song or call, call or song? Many birds, including this male northern cardinal, use songs to attract mates or claim territory and use calls to communicate with one another about food or danger.

Open wide—and sing! This western meadowlark sings about 10 different songs. Eastern meadowlarks look similar, but sing between 50 and 100 songs!

Baby birds are born knowing their species' calls, but they have to learn the songs by listening to father birds around them. At first young birds just jabber a "sort of" song—bird baby talk. But eventually they learn how to sing as well as grownups.

Listen carefully to the birds making music in your mornings. Pick a simple one and try to whistle it yourself. Can you learn to sing like a bird?

dawn watch:
recording the performance

To make a "record" of the morning bird concert, all you need are a tape recorder (and a microphone if your recorder doesn't have one), a blank tape, a watch, and an alarm clock. Set the clock for one hour before sunrise.

When you wake up, dress in warm clothes and go outdoors with your tape recorder and your watch. Turn the recorder on, say what time it is, and let the recorder run for about five minutes. Then turn it off and wait 10 minutes before turning it on, saying the time, and recording for another five minutes. Keep recording this way until sunrise, or for as long as you want.

Listen to your recording. Do different birds sing at different times? Do the songs change? Compare your recording to tapes or CDs of birdsongs at your library. Can you figure out what kinds of birds you recorded?

Like many other birds, this Bell's vireo sings its musical song over and over again to attract a mate.

was beethoven's fifth a wren's first?

Many great musical composers have used morning birdsongs for inspiration. Mozart wrote birdsongs into his music and publicly thanked his pet starling for giving him ideas. The famous opening notes of Beethoven's Fifth Symphony are the same as the song of the white-breasted wood wren.

133

dew drink up

When the air around this spider web cooled at night, it couldn't hold as much water vapor, so it let go of the extra water and sprinkled the web with dewdrops.

Have you ever walked outdoors on a bright, early morning and found everything sparkling with tiny droplets of water—dew? Sometimes there's so much dew your shoes get soaked when you walk through grass. Dew does more than just get your feet wet, though. It's an important source of fresh water for birds and animals (in deserts, it's sometimes the *only* source). Raccoons and other mammals lick the moisture from plant leaves. Salmanders absorb the dampness through their skin. Birds sip dew collected in little pools in tree hollows and flower blossoms. Some birds give themselves morning showers by shaking the dew off leafy branches.

In other words, without dew many creatures would be done for. But where does all the early morning water come from? Answer: the night—or, at least, the coolness that night brings.

To see how this happens, just fill a glass with ice and water on a warm day and wait about 30 minutes.

Presto, droplets of water—dew—appear on the outside of the glass. Why? Because the icy glass made the air around it a bit cooler. All air contains water in the form of a gas, or *vapor*. But cold air can't hold as much water vapor as warm air. So the glass-chilled air let go of some of the water. The water vapor *condensed* into drops of liquid water that collected on the glass surface.

That's what also happens outside on clear, still nights. Without the sun's warmth, the ground loses its heat. The air near the ground becomes cooler and can't hold as much water vapor. So the water vapor condenses and collects on the ground and things near it: grass, leaves, flowers, spider webs, and—uh oh, did you leave this book outside last night?

make a night and day study plot

Make a tiny piece of Planet Earth your own and study the plants and creatures living there. You'll see some amazing changes, so different they're like— night and day.

what you need

An area about 3 x 3 feet (0.9 x 0.9 m) in a yard or field

Tape measure

Hammer

Tent stakes or wooden sticks

Twine

Magnifying glass or hand lens

Notebook

Pencil

Field guides

Flashlight

Camera

what to do

1 Choose a place to study where there's a variety of plants, some tall, some short, some flowering, some not. An area at the edge of a lawn or field is usually good.

2 Once you've chosen an interesting area, use the tape to measure off a plot 3 feet square (0.9 m²). Hammer a stake or stick into the ground at each corner of the square. Then tie twine between the stakes, connecting them, to make a marked-off study plot (see the photos on the next page). Be sure to drive the stakes firmly into the ground so the twine won't pull them loose.

3 Think of the marked-off area as a tiny world all by itself. Never mind everything around it. Look carefully at just the plants and creatures inside the string. At first your study plot will seem sort of ordinary and maybe even boring. But be patient. Give yourself five or 10 minutes to start noticing what makes your study plot special. Do you see ants or other insects crawling along the ground? Imagine what the

plot would look like to you if you were that small and walking the same path. The grass would be 15 times taller than you. And the taller plants would seem like huge trees!

4 How many different kinds of plants live in your study-plot world? Notice the different leaf shapes and where each kind of plant is in the plot. Do you find any mushrooms? Spider webs? What else is on the ground? Do you see nutshells or seeds? Beetles?

5 The closer you look, the more you'll see. Use a magnifying glass or hand lens to check out the insides of flowers and the undersides of leaves for teensy insects (yikes; they look like monsters!). Peer through the grass to the soil surface below. Are there any earthworm holes?

6 Write down your observations in the notebook. Use field guides to help you figure out the names of your world's plants and creatures.

7 Once you've gotten to know your study plot during the day, you can start noticing its night-and-day differences. Visit the plot at the

same times each morning and night (either just before dark or with a flashlight after dark).

Night and day differences to look for:

Are there different numbers or kinds of creatures?

Is there dew on the plants?

Are the flowers open or closed?

Do some kinds of plants raise or lower their leaves? (Hint: watch the clover.)

8 The longer you study your roped-off world, the more you'll learn. What night and day changes are different as the seasons change? How much do your plants grow? Take photographs of your plot every week or so. Compare your first photos and notes with later ones.

what puts the color in sunsets?

Sunsets and sunrises can be spectacular light shows. The sky and clouds near the horizon glow with pinks, reds, and oranges. Where does the color come from?

You probably already know that sunlight, or "white light," is actually made up of seven different colors: red, orange, yellow, green, blue, indigo, and violet. These make up the *spectrum*—the colors you see in a rainbow. Maybe you've even used a three-sided piece of glass or plastic, called a *prism*, to separate sunlight into the colors of the spectrum.

You might also know that light travels in the form of waves and that each color in the spectrum has a different wavelength. Blue,

for instance, has a short wavelength. Red and orange have long wavelengths.

On its way from the Sun to us, sunlight has to pass through Earth's atmosphere. When it does, colors with short wavelengths, especially blue, are separated and scattered in all directions by air molecules, water vapor, and other particles. That's why the sky looks blue to us during the day, when the Sun is high. The blue is scattered everywhere. Colors with long wavelengths aren't

separated from sunlight as easily by air particles, so we don't usually see them.

At dawn and dusk, though, when the Sun is low, light has to travel farther through the atmosphere to reach our eyes. By the time that happens, all the blue and other short-wavelength colors have been scattered away, and only the red, orange, and sometimes yellow are left. Result: Wow! What a beautiful sunrise! What a gorgeous sunset!

how the sun colors the edges of night

At sunrise and sunset, the sunlight we see has traveled farther through the atmosphere than the light we see at midday. Much of the blue has been scattered away by air molecules and particles by the

Sun high during day

short distance

Sun low at sunrise and sunset

long distance

time the light reaches our eyes. We see mostly the remaining reds and oranges.

atmosphere

sunset-to-sunrise night sounds clock

what you need

An old 33 rpm vinyl record

Piece of paper larger than the record

Pencil

Ruler

Medium- or fine-grit sandpaper

Paper plates

Acrylic paints in orange, light purple,
   blue, navy blue, yellow

Paintbrushes (small and large)

Glow-in-the-dark paint,
   natural or white

Metallic marker pens, gold and silver

Black foam core board,
   20 x 20 inches (50.8 x 50.8 cm)

Battery-powered clockwork kit
   (sold at craft stores) with
   ¼-inch (6 mm) shaft

Multipurpose glue

Scissors

Shiny mirror paper
   (sold at craft stores)

AA batteries

Magazines with photos of birds
   and animals

Pushpins

There's something strange about this clock: it's upside down! Most clocks have "12" at the top to mark midnight, the beginning of a new 24-hour day. This one has "6" at the top to mark the beginning of the night, from dusk (6 PM) to dawn (6 AM). What special nature sounds do you hear at dusk, during the night, and at dawn? Listen carefully, then cut out photos of the creatures you think are making the sounds and pin them to the clock next to the times you hear them.

what to do

1 Put the record on top of the paper and trace around it with the pencil. Remove the record but keep the circle and paper in front of you. The circle will help you figure out where to put the clock's numbers.

2 Use the ruler and pencil to draw a straight line from the top to the bottom of the circle, where 6 o'clock (at the top) and 12 o'clock (at the bottom) will be on the clock. Draw another line straight across the circle, where 9 and 3 o'clock will be. Next, along the edge of each of the four "pie" shapes you've drawn, make two marks equally spaced. When you've done this with all four pie shapes, you'll have marked all the positions of the hours (see the photo, left). Mark their numbers on the *outside* of the circle, starting with 6 at the top, and working clockwise: 7, 8, 9, and so on.

3 Rub one side of the record with the sandpaper to scratch it up. Paint will stick better to the roughed-up plastic.

4 Put the record back in place on the circle, with the numbers showing on the paper. Using the ruler and pencil, draw one line from the center of the record to the edge at the 5 o'clock mark and another line from the center to 7 o'clock. This wedge, between 5 o'clock and 7 o'clock, roughly represents the edges of night around sunrise and sunset. Set the paper and circle aside for now.

5 On a paper plate, mix some orange paint with a little bit of light purple to give it a deeper color. Try to create a color that reminds you of the colors of the sky at dawn and dusk.

6 Now, using one of the larger brushes, brush the orange-purple mixture over the wedge you drew between the 5 o'clock and 7 o'clock lines.

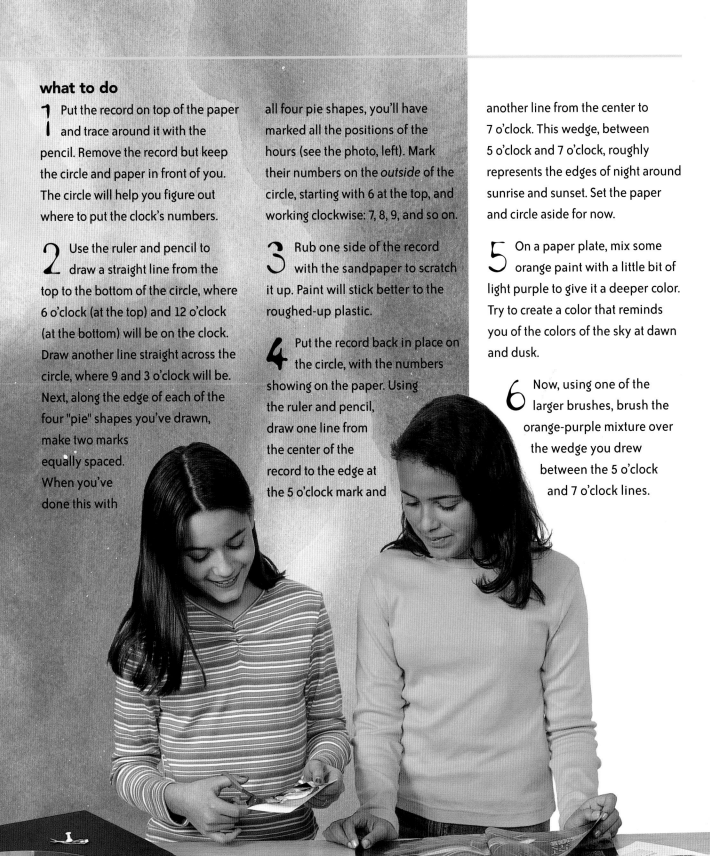

7 With the second large paintbrush, paint a mixture of blue and navy blue over the rest of the record to the rim. Use more of the lighter blue closer to the sunrise and sunset lines and more of the navy blue toward the bottom half of the record. Let the paint dry overnight.

8 When all the paint has dried, use yellow paint and a small brush to paint a half-sun shape in the bottom of the orange-purple wedge. Use glow-in-the-dark paint and the second small brush to paint a moon shape and stars on the blue part of the record (see the photo on page 138).

9 Use the silver metallic marker pen to outline the moon, the stars, and the rim of the record's blue section. Use the gold pen to outline the rim and the borders of the orange-purple wedge. Let all the paint dry completely.

10 Put the record back over the circle on the paper and use a pencil to lightly mark the positions of the numbers on the record. Use the gold pen to write the number 6 on the record at the top, and the silver pen to write the numbers 3, 9, and 12 in their positions. Be sure to make them large enough to read from a distance. Then use the gold and silver pens to make small wedge marks (see the photo) at the other number positions—or, if you'd rather, just write those numbers on the record, too.

11 Center the record on top of the square of foam core board. While holding the record in place, put a sharpened pencil into the hole in the record's center and poke it through the foam core below to make a hole big enough for the clock shaft.

12 Squeeze some glue onto the back of the record and around the center of the foam core square. Set the record in place, with the center hole over the hole you poked, and press it against the foam core.

13 The clockwork kit will include a base with a shaft (which turns the hands), plus the hands and parts to attach them. Squeeze some glue onto the clockwork base, slip the shaft through the holes in the foam core and record, and press the base against the foam core board until the glue dries. Then attach the hands to the shaft on the night-clock side, following the instructions that came with the kit.

14 To make the hands on your clock easier to see, cut larger hand shapes from a sheet of metallic silver mirror paper to fit over the metal clock hands. Glue the paper hands over the metal ones.

15 Install the batteries, hang your new clock on a wall, and start listening for night sounds. Every time you hear something new, find a photo of it in a magazine, cut it out, and tack it with a pushpin near the time you heard the sound. Soon all sorts of night creatures will be hanging out around your clock.

good night!

At dusk, some of the day birds that sang in the morning sing again, just to make sure: "I'm *still* here! This is *still* my place!" Gradually, as the sun sets and daylight fades, those birds rest and night birds take over. Screech owls whistle their high, eerie call. Great horned owls hoot. Nighthawks soar the sky crying *peet, peet*.

But soon a different sort of chorus rings through the darkening night: the chiming, chirping songs of insects, frogs, and toads. It's time for night creatures to call for mates and claim their territory. At first, the sounds might seem to blend together into one big racket. But listen carefully. Focus on just one kind of sound at a time. How many different sounds can you count? Can you pick out the frog and toad sounds from the insects?

Dusk is a good time to watch for early signs of larger nightlife, too. Can you figure out which creatures come out first and which ones later? As darkness falls, mice start to skitter beneath the leaves. Raccoons leave their hiding places. Opossums waddle along the edges of lawns, sniffing for food. And look—over near the bushes by that house's back door, an interesting two-legged creature has just come out with a red-beamed flashlight. It's quietly walking, stopping, listening, watching. It must be—yes, it *is:* a night explorer!

acknowledgments

What an amazing privilege it is to receive so much help from so many good and talented people. I especially want to thank:

Stacey Budge, this book's art director, for her humor, patience, creativity, keen sense of design, and can-do spirit. They show in every page.

Joe Rhatigan, for his unflagging generosity with insight, advice, and encouragement.

Heather Smith, for her enthusiasm and support even at times when she had good reason to bow out. Heather was instrumental in the concept and planning of this book, and wrote the activities Be A Bat (Moth!) (page 65) and Disappearing Heads (page 25). She also designed the Eye-Shine Mask (page 15), Bat-Wing Kite (page 66), Moon Catcher (page 129), and Night Sounds Clock (page 138).

Veronika Gunter and Cindy Burda, for their persistence in helping me locate photos and pin down pesky details.

Carlton Burke, exhibits curator at the Western North Carolina Nature Center, for his wonderful kid-friendly designs for the Bat House (page 60) and Screech Owl House (page 76).

Diana Light, project designer extraordinaire and creator of the Night Blind (page 22).

Scott Weidensaul, author of *Living on the Wind* and *The Ghost with Trembling Wings* (North Point Press), for his expert counsel on bird migration.

Keith Sutton, editor of *Arkansas Wildlife* magazine, for helping me find such highly skilled wildlife photographers.

Steve and Dave Maslowski and Joe and Mary Ann McDonald—the aforementioned highly skilled wildlife photographers. Also David H. Funk, for his extraordinary insect photography. I'm honored to share these pages with you.

Marcianne Miller and Andy Rae, for making me laugh. Thank you both, my friends.

All the wonderful, funny, silly, smart, talented, hard-working, cooperative kids who modeled for this book and brought so much energy to our photo shoots:

Matt Anderson, Kia Baden, Jordan Brendle, Caitlyn Caskey, Aja Cobbs, Cody Griffin, Summer Griffin, Leah Haile, Terry Lonergan, Daniel Luna, Corrina Matthews, Natasha Perez, Andy Rae (grownup kid), J.J. Peterson, Ray Peterson, Noah Ratner, Gus Rowan, Mali Rowan, Addison Smith, Phillip Treadway, Alex Villarreal, Jasmine Villarreal, Dylan Wolhart, Kayla Wolhart

photo credits

Steve and Dave Maslowski: pages 2,
  3, 23, 38, 39, 41 (lower right), 42,
  45, 47 (upper left), 48 (upper right),
  50 (upper left), 59 (upper left),
  69, 72, 81 (lower left), 82, 84,
  85 (upper left), 102, 105, 131, 134

McDonald Wildlife Photography:
  pages 11, 27 (right), 40,
  41 (upper left), 43, 46,
  47 (lower right), 48 (lower left),
  56, 58, 70 (upper left), 71, 73,
  76 (lower right), 81 (upper right),
  100 (upper left)

David H. Funk: pages 5 (middle left),
  85 (right, top and bottom), 86,
  87 (middle right, top and bottom),
  92, 99, 100 (middle),
  101 (left and middle),
  104 (upper left)

Evan Bracken: 24, 25, 34, 54, 55, 103

Robert Miller: 107 (lower right)

Brand X Pictures: 5 (top right),
  87 (lower left and upper right),
  98, 100 (upper right), 101 (right),
  106 (upper right)

Courtesy of NASA: 108, 110, 111, 112,
  116, 117, 118, 119, 120 (upper left),
  122, 125, 127, 128 (upper left)

Courtesy of U.S. Fish and Wildlife
  Service (photographer credited):
  pages 5 (bottom; Gary M. Stolz),
  88 (James Leupold), 123 (Richard
  A. Coon), 132 (John and Karen
  Hollingworth), 133 (Steve
  Maslowski), 137 (Anna Ramsburg),
  140 (Gary M. Stolz)

Back cover credits:
Foreground, John Widman;
  background, USFWS
  (Richard A. Coon)
Inset photos (top to bottom):
  USFWS (James Leupold),
  John Widman, NASA,
  USFWS (Steve Maslowski)

index